Table of Contents

1 | GATEWAY TO GO

2 | An Easy Toolkit with 5 Lessons

About 'Gateway to Go'

The purpose of this book is to make learning and
enjoying Go accessible to everyone through five short lessons.
Its purpose also is to contribute to the spread of
a community that enjoys Go, supporting the mission of
"Go For A Better World," which is to promote Go and prevent dementia.

The planning for this book was undertaken by Jake Kim,
founder of "Go For A Better World," a nonprofit organization started
in the United States that has recently opened operations in Korea.
To fulfill the mission of reducing the risk of dementia through the expansion of Go,
"Go For A Better World," in collaboration with "DoDream Education,"
which is a Go education specialist, developed this book.
Through learning and playing Go, both organizations
believe cognitive functions, social interactions, and emotional
well-being will be enhanced, thus contributing to dementia prevention.

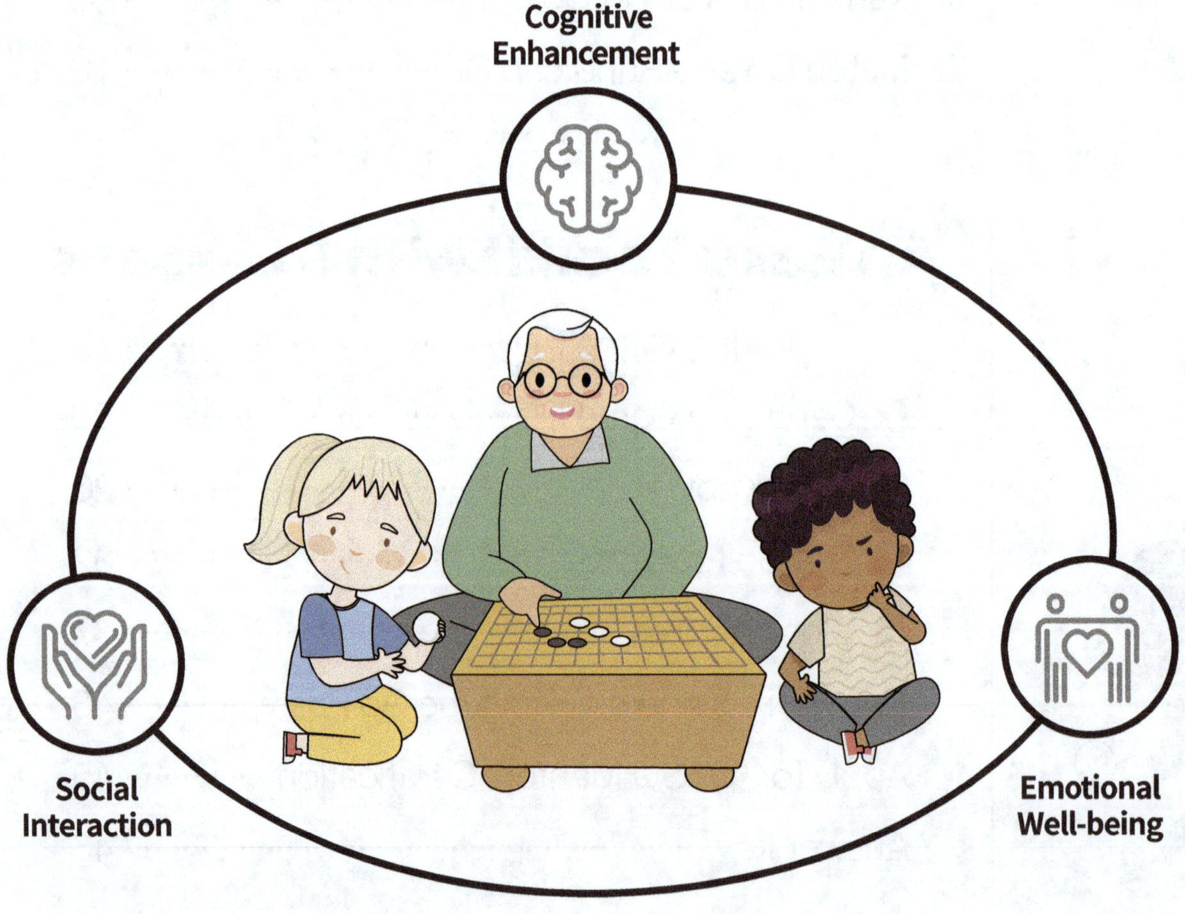

Go: A Game of Wisdom and Strategy

Go is a board game believed to have been invented
around 4,000 years ago during China's Taiping Civilization,
also known as the Yao Dynasty.

The first game of Go was said to have been
created by a king for the purpose of educating a foolish prince.

Later, it is said that the son,
having learned wisdom through Go,
used it to govern the country wisely.

Go Around the World

Go has developed primarily in Asian countries such as Korea, China, Taiwan, and Japan, which continue to dominate the professional Go leagues. There is, however, a vibrant community of Go enthusiasts in countries around the world, including the United States, Canada, Mexico, Argentina, France and Italy, where people learn and enjoy the game.

The US Go Congress and EU Go Congress are held annually in the United States and Europe, respectively, bringing hundreds of Go enthusiasts together from around the world.

The largest Go tournament, in terms of prize money, is the Ing Cup, established by Taiwanese tycoon Ing Chang-ki in 1988. Held every four years, it has a large prize pool and is sometimes referred to as the "Go Olympics" or "Go World Cup."

Is Go considered a sport? Go is recognized as a mind sport, and it was adopted as an official event at the Asian Games in 2010 and 2022. It has become the venue where players from different Asian countries compete.

Go and AI

In March 2016, a historic Go match took place between
renowned Korean Go player, Lee Sedol 9-Dan, and the top artificial
intelligence Go program, AlphaGo.

The match consisted of five games with a total prize of $1 million.
It garnered worldwide attention. The competition sparked debate
between predictions that machines would find it
difficult to overcome the near-infinite possibilities of Go and that AlphaGo,
with its application of deep learning, had already surpassed
human capabilities. In the end, AlphaGo won 4 games to 1,
leading to the mainstreaming of artificial intelligence Go programs.
Since then, the Go community has been utilizing various AI Go programs
in training, leading to an overall improvement in skill levels.

Go Game Tools

Go is a game that can be enjoyed with simple tools - a Go board
and black and white Go markers known as stones.
The specifications of the Go board and stones used in official
Go games are as follows:

Go Board

- Consists of 19 horizontal lines and 19 vertical lines.
- The board measures 42cm in width and 45cm in height.
- Contains a total of 361 intersections or crossing points.
  * There are 13x13 and 9x9 Go boards available for beginners.

Go Stones

- Consist of black stones and white stones(Black plays first).
- The black stones consist of 181 pieces,
  and the white stones consist of 180 pieces.
- During a game, captured stones are stored in the lid of capturer's Go bowl.

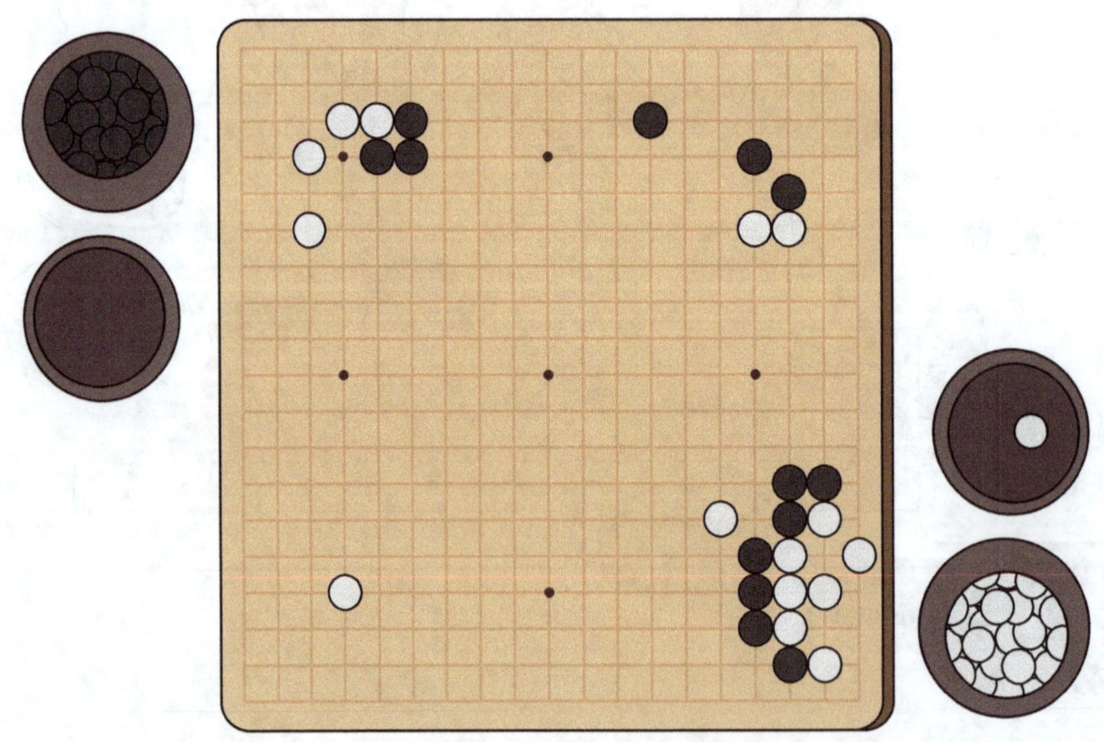

The Flow of a Game of Go

Go is a game where two players take turns placing white
and black stones. Ultimately, the player who secures
the most territory wins. The flow of a game of Go typically starts
with early territorial expansion, proceeds to mid-game battles,
and concludes with solidifying territory in the late game.

Stage	Game Strategy	Game Tactics*
Early Game	Occupy advantageous positions first.	Hanema, Joseki
Mid-Early Game	Expand your territory.	Opening
Mid Game	Assess the situation of the opponent's stones and our stones.	Position evaluation, Crucial spot
Late-Mid Game	Execute planned strategies and tactics.	Capturing race, Life-and-Death
Late Game	Expand your territory until the end.	Endgame

* This book focuses on the basic concepts of Go, and does not cover
the tactical aspect of the game. After completing the introductory lessons of
"Gateway to Go," you can learn the tactics of Go to enhance your skills.

Determining the Outcome of a Go Game

In Go, the game concludes with a process called "scoring."
The winner and loser are determined based on the
confirmed territory and captured stones.
Here is the method for determining the outcome of a Go game:

1. Carefully check if there are any more places to play.
2. Fill in the empty intersections between black and white stones alternately to complete the "dame" (neutral points).
3. Ask the opponent if they want to proceed to the scoring phase.
4. Remove "dead stones" from the board.
5. Use the captured stones and the dead stones to fill the opponent's territory.
6. Arrange the territory in a square or rectangular shape using multiples of 5 or 10 stones to create a clear shape.
7. Each player counts the number of territory points they have.

Ranking System in Go

The ranking system in Go is known as the "Dan-Kyu system," which numerically represents an individual's skill level in the game. In this system, a lower number indicates a higher skill level for "Kyu" ranks, while a higher number indicates a higher skill level for "Dan" ranks.

Go is divided into amateur and professional levels. Amateur players start from a "Kyu" rank and progress to a "Dan" rank. If you complete the 5 introductory lessons in this book, you should easily pass Amateur 25 Kyu.

Professional Go players are those who have passed the professional qualification exam and entered the professional ranks as a 1-Dan professional, competing in professional Go tournaments against other professional players. In professional Go, 9-Dan is the highest rank, as in the case of "Lee Sedol 9-Dan."

	AMATEUR	PROFESSIONAL
Kyu Ranks	30 Kyu to 1 Kyu	N/A
Dan Ranks	1 Dan to 7 Dan	1 Dan to 9 Dan

Match Go and Handicap Go

Match Go and Handicap Go are forms of Go where players of different skill levels play against each other. Match Go is played between players of similar skill levels and comes in two forms:

- Even Match Go: After a "stone covering" game where the players decide who plays as black and white, the white player starts with a 6.5 point komi (bonus points),known as Hoseon.
- Handicap Match Go: Players start without a "stone covering" game and the black player starts without komi, known as Jeongseon.

Handicap Go, on the other hand, is played between players with significant ranking difference where the weaker player takes black and receives a predetermined number of black stones on the board to start, based on the ranks of the players.

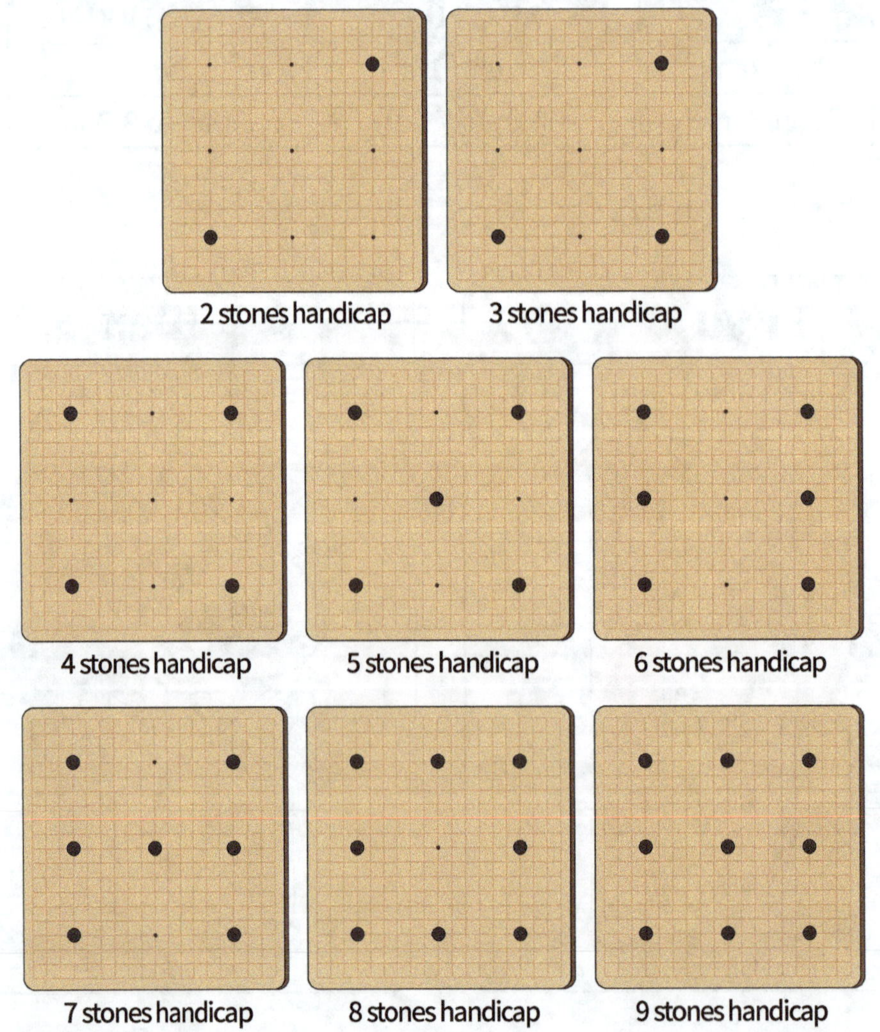

2 stones handicap   3 stones handicap

4 stones handicap   5 stones handicap   6 stones handicap

7 stones handicap   8 stones handicap   9 stones handicap

Gateway to Go
An Easy Toolkit with 5 Lessons

Go For A Better World

Capturing Game I

Liberty
The free intersections around a stone that are not occupied by other stones.

Capturing
Placing a stone to make the opponent's stones have no liberties.

Saving
Placing a stone to increase the liberties of your own stones.

🐺 Liberty

🐺 Capturing

🐺 Saving

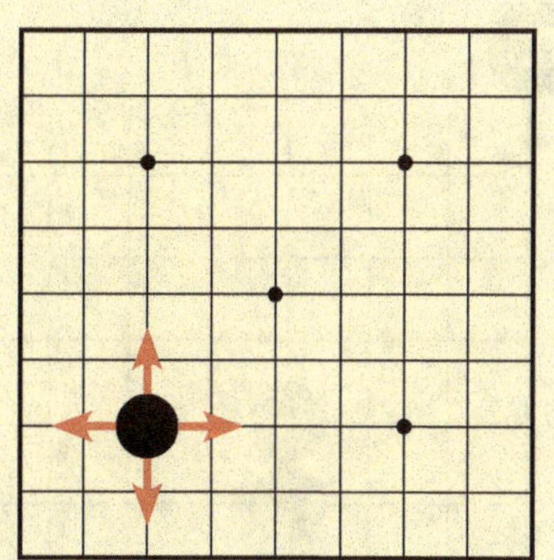

01 Free intersections that a stone has and not occupied by other stones.

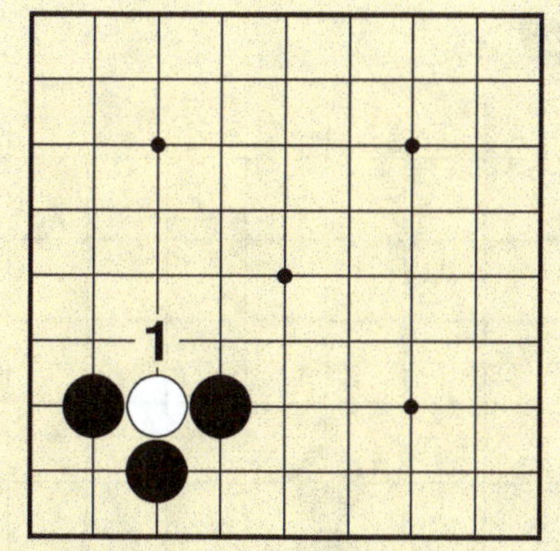

01 A white stone has one liberty.

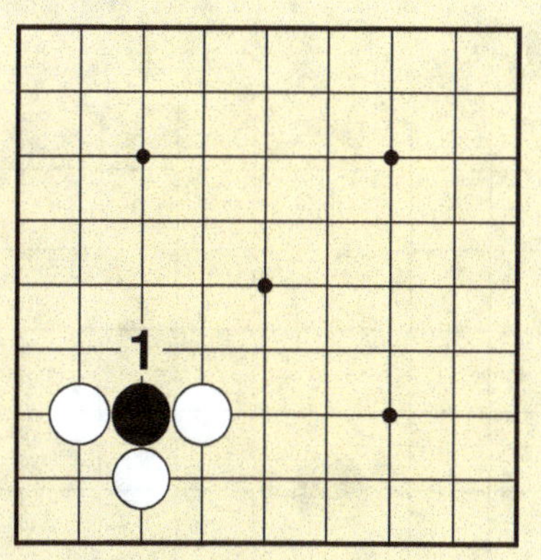

01 A black stone has one liberty.

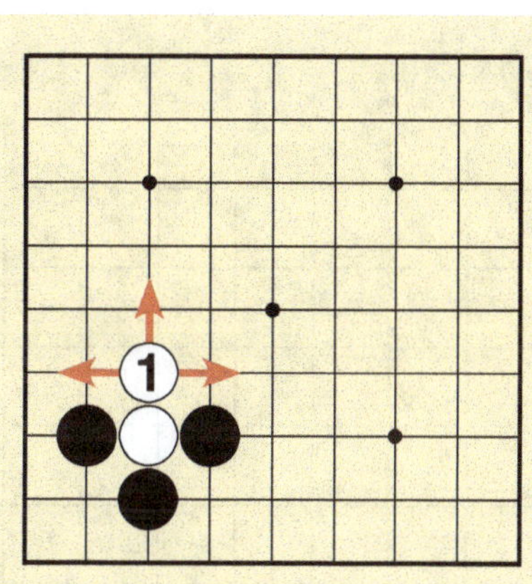

02 Free intersections not connected to a stone are not considered liberties.

02 If white moves first, it gains more liberties.

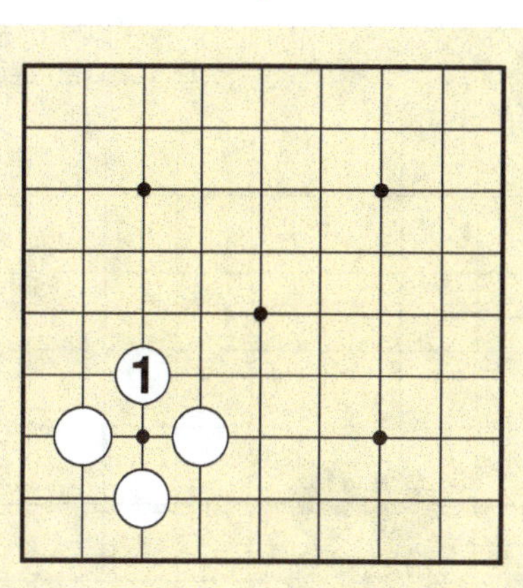

02 If white places a stone (White 1) first, it blocks all liberties of the black stone, capturing it.

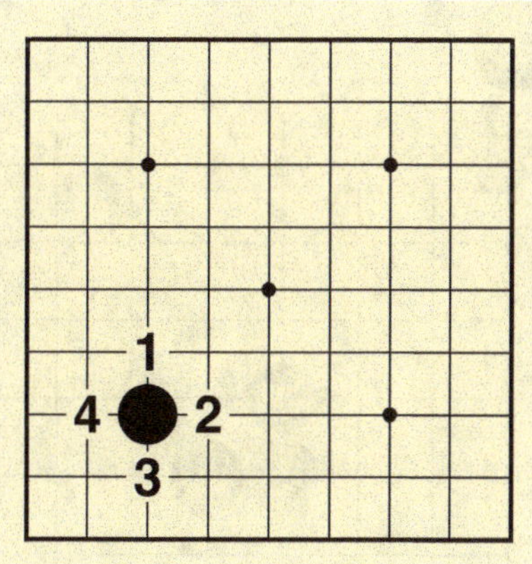

03 Count the number of liberties a stone has.

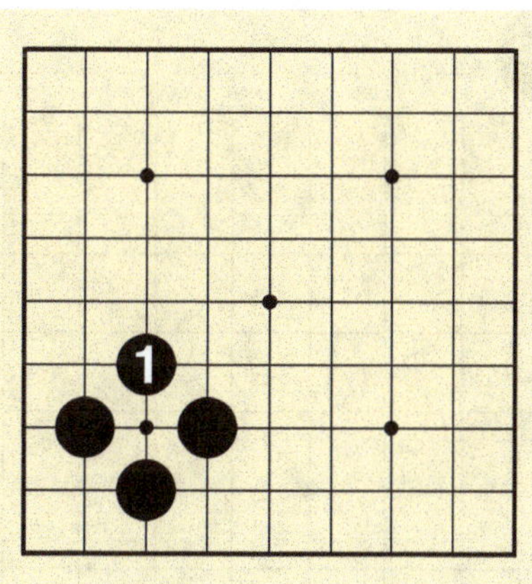

03 Place a black stone (Black 1) to capture the white stone by occupying its last liberty.

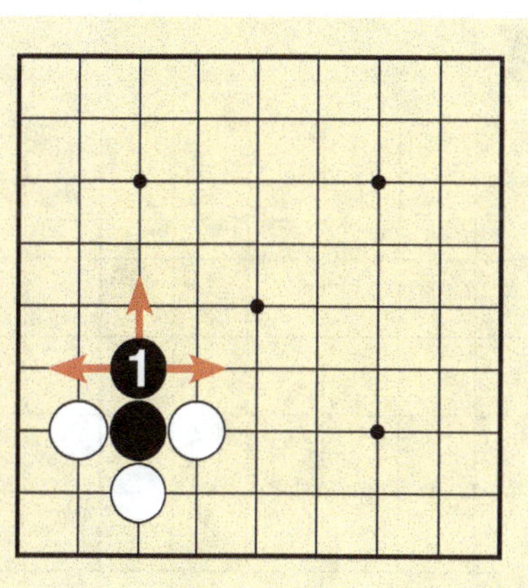

03 Place a black stone (Black 1) to save the black stone by increasing its liberties.

? **Find and count the liberties of black stones.**

01

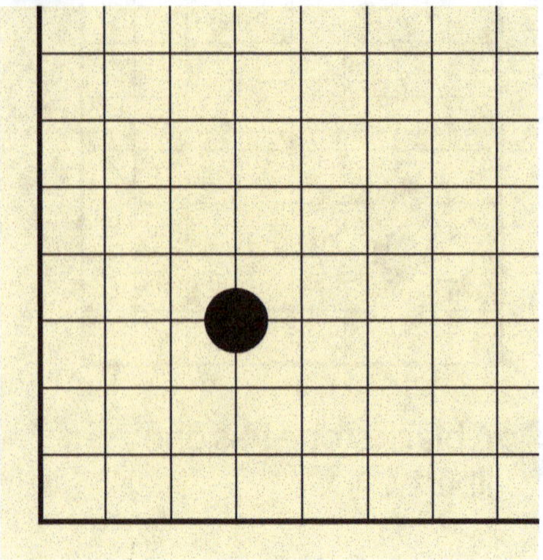

02

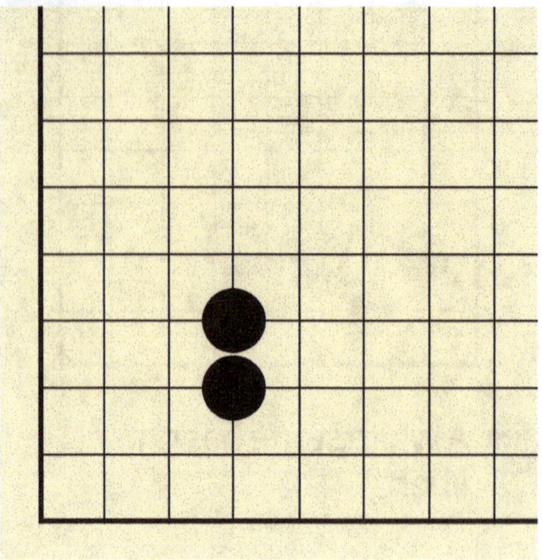

03

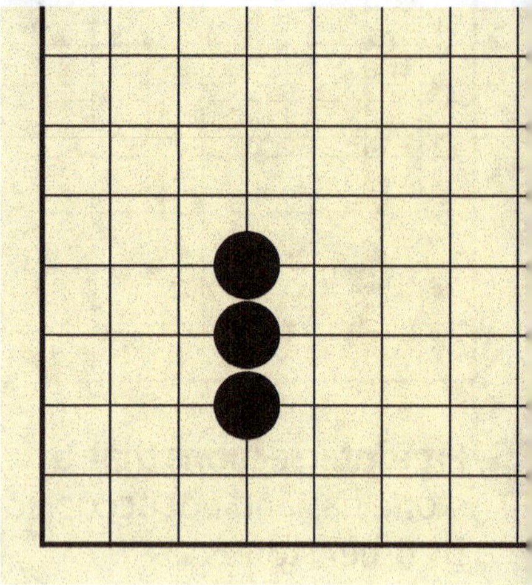

04

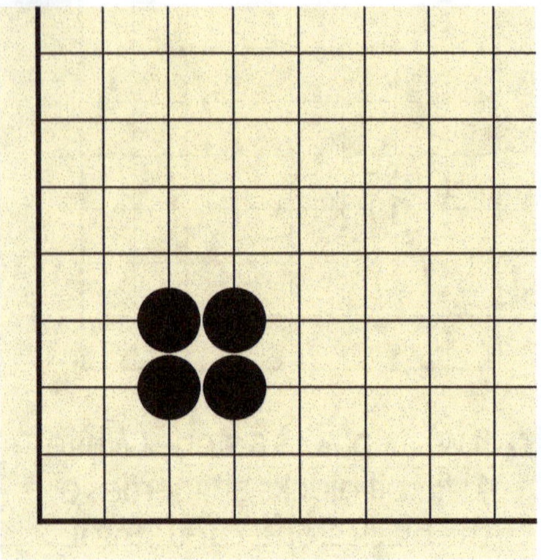

05

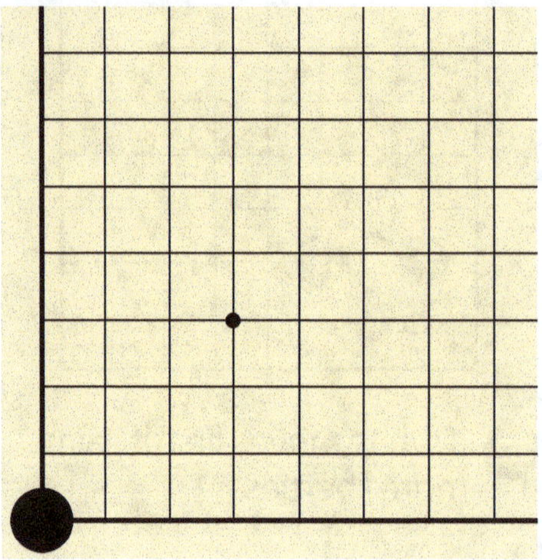

06

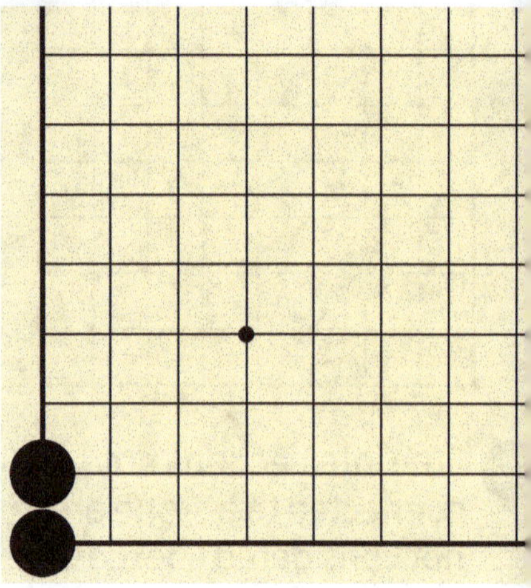

07

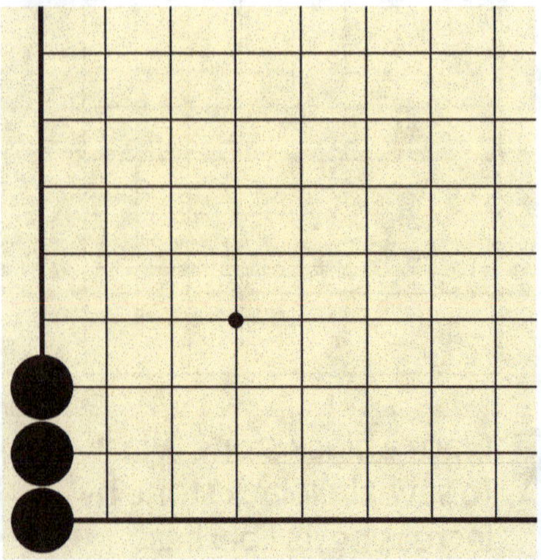

08

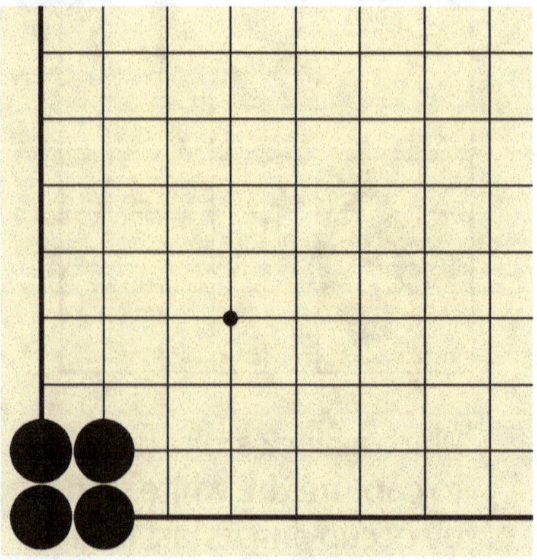

09

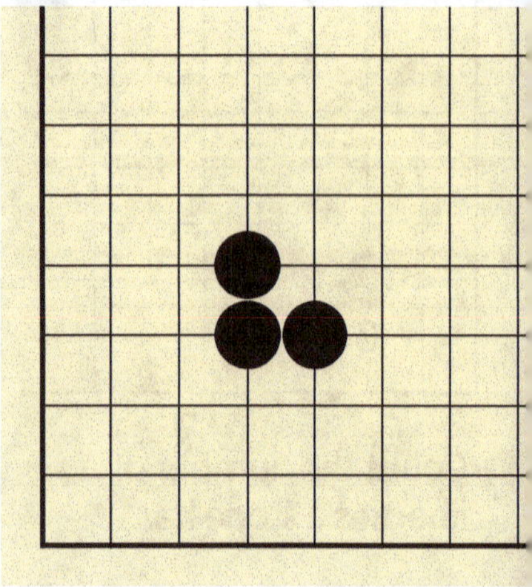

1 Capturing Game I _ 1 Liberty

Black's Turn

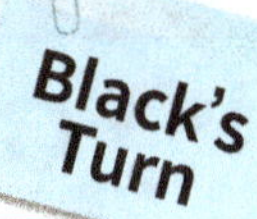

? Find and count the liberties of black stones.

10

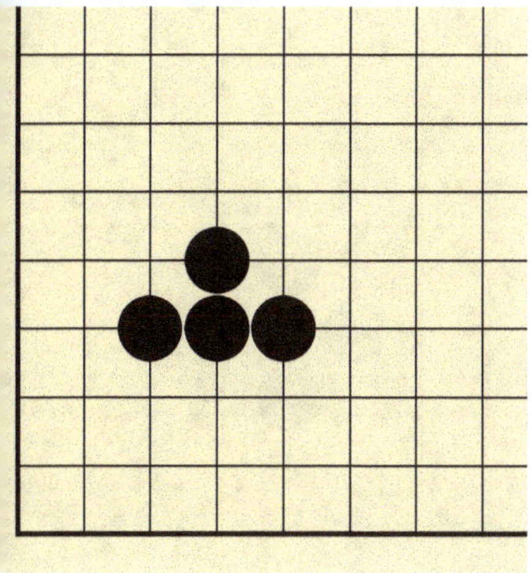

11

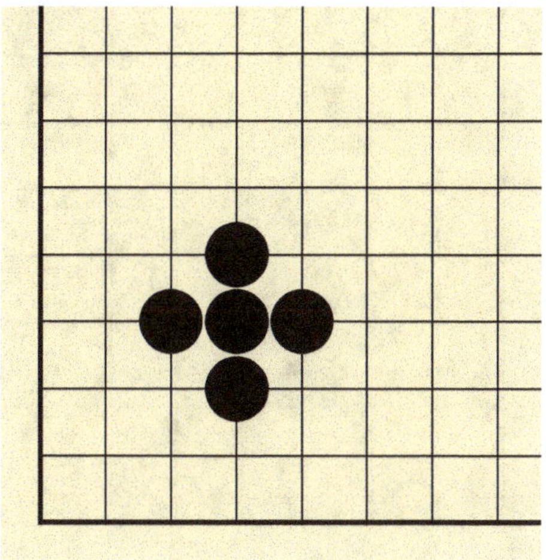

12

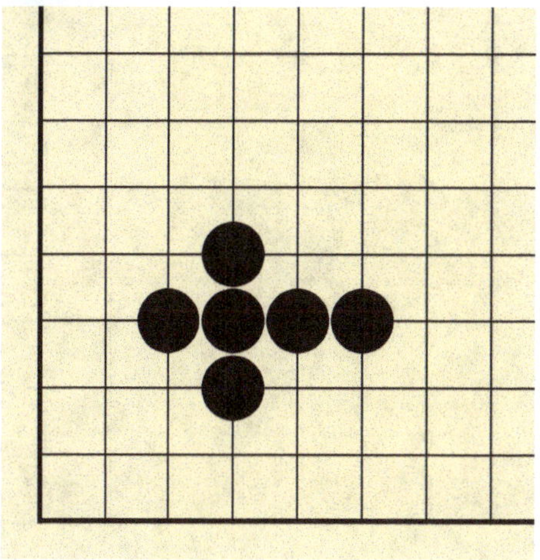

13

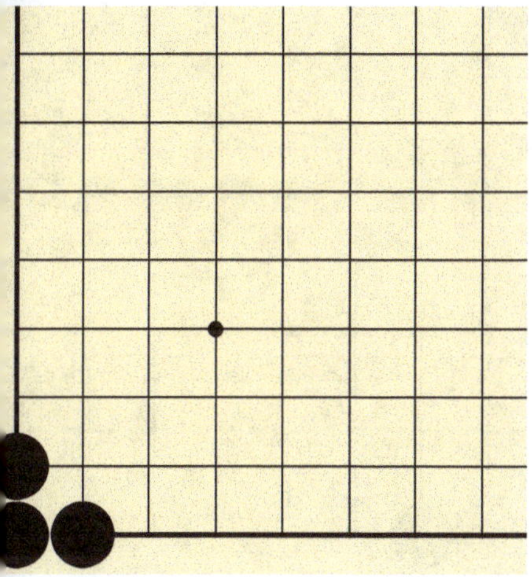

14

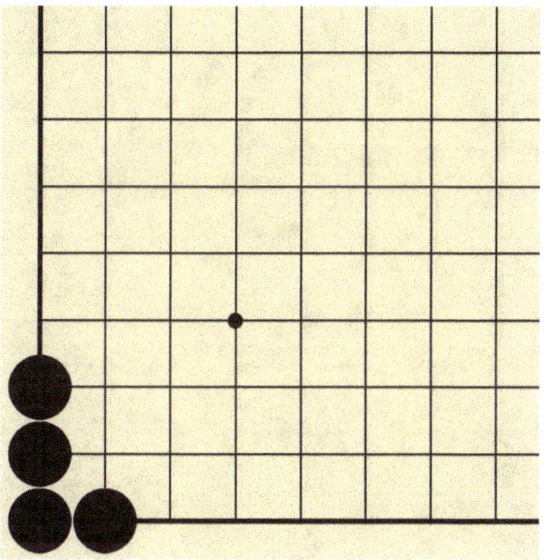

15

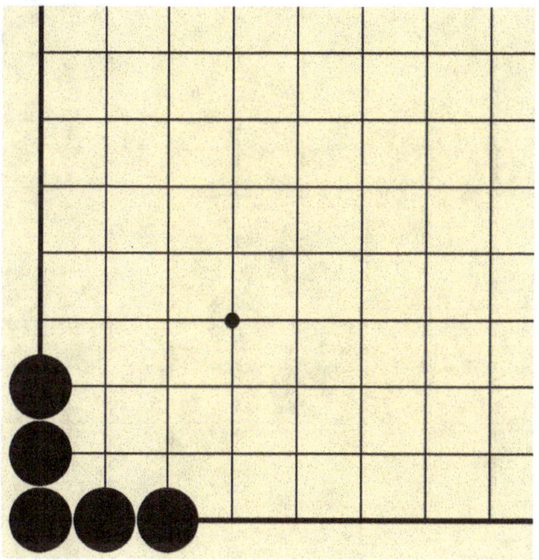

16

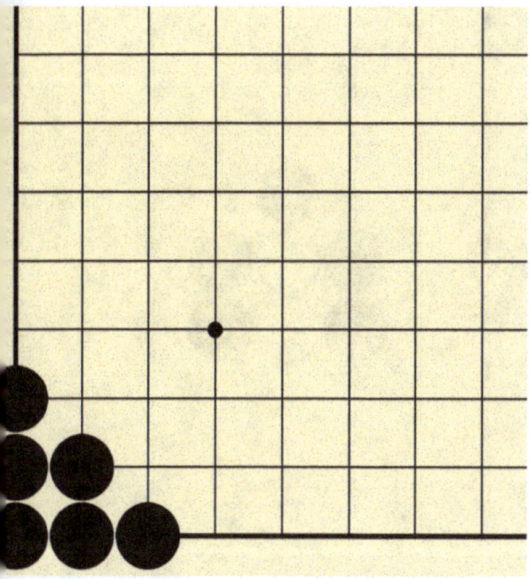

17

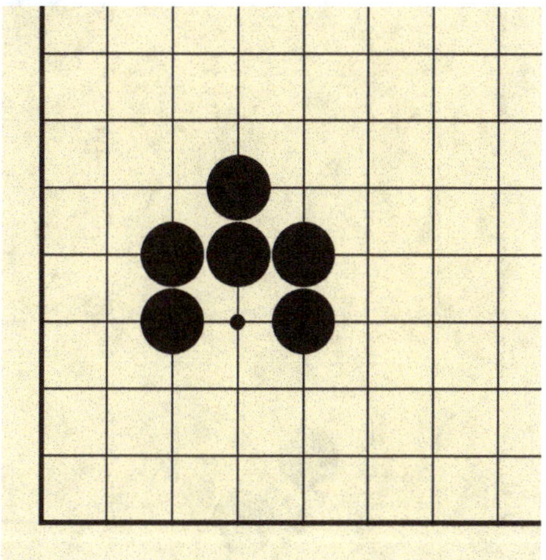

18

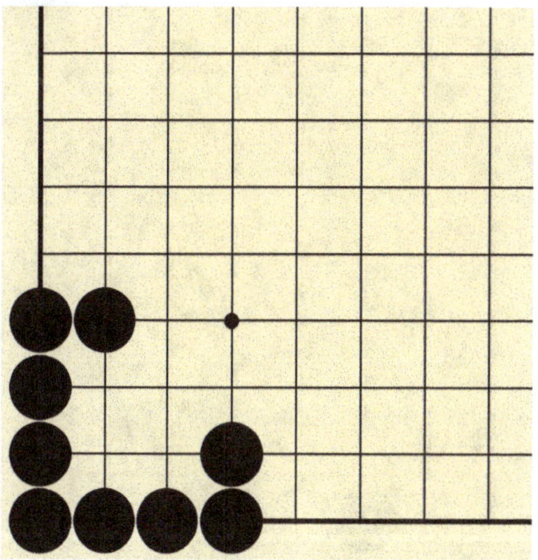

1 Capturing Game I _ 2 Capturing

Black's Turn

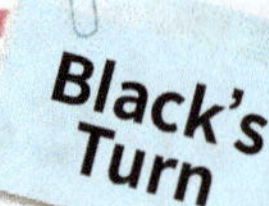

? Capture the white stones.

01

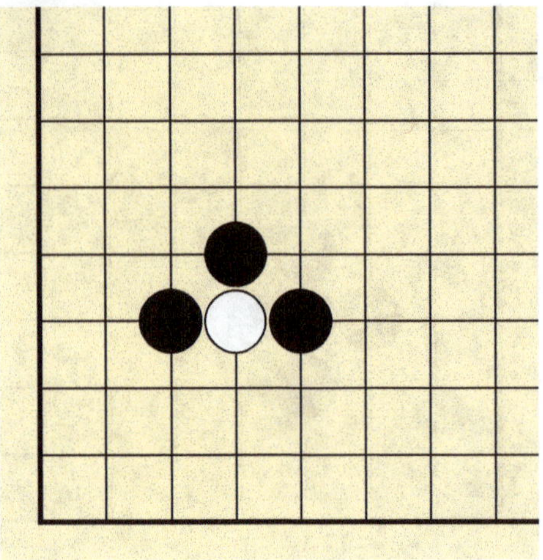

02

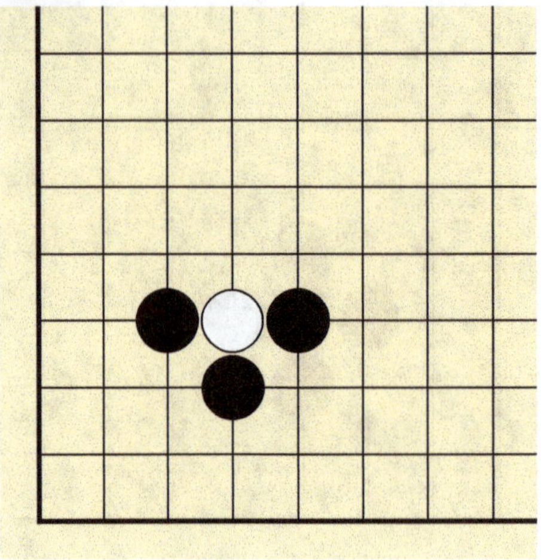

03

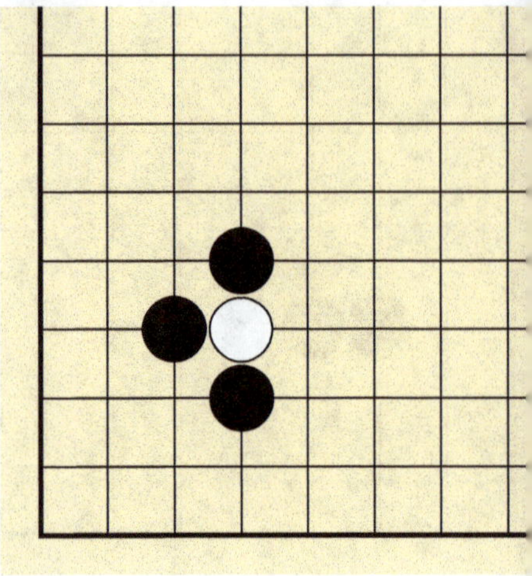

04

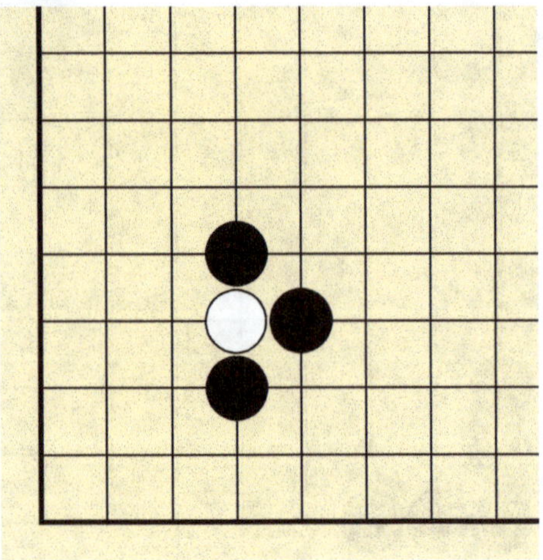

05

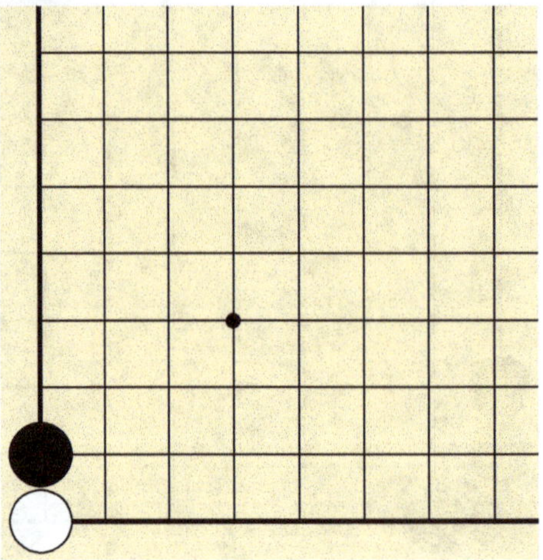

06

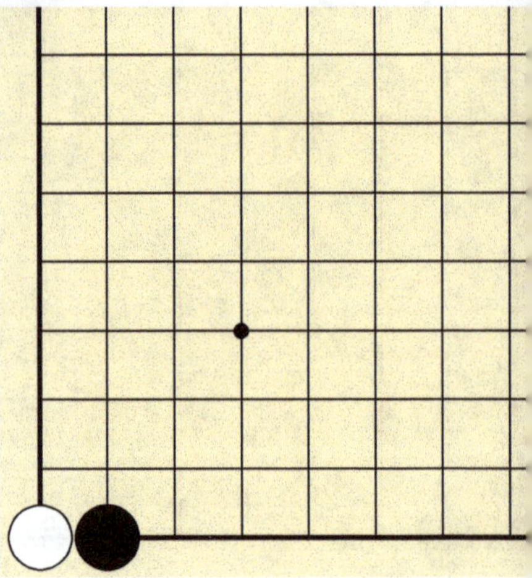

07

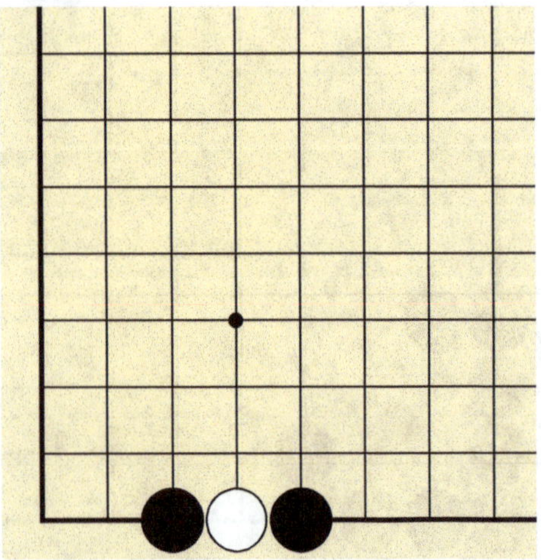

08

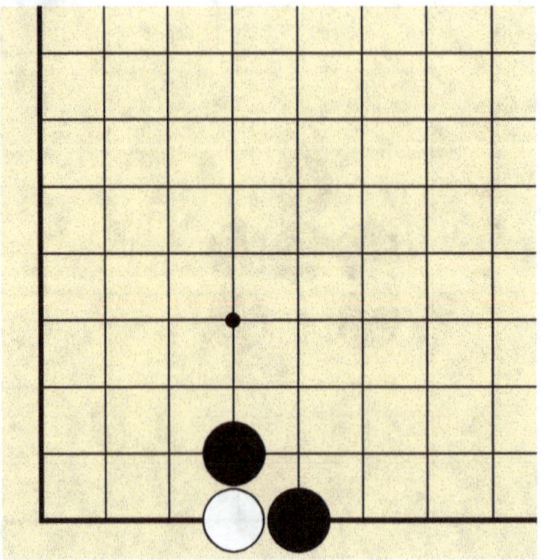

09

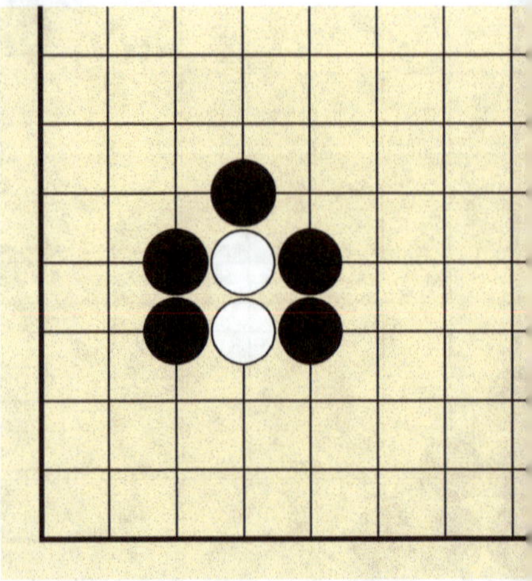

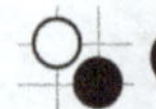

❶ Capturing Game I _ ❷ Capturing

Black's Turn

? Capture the white stones.

0

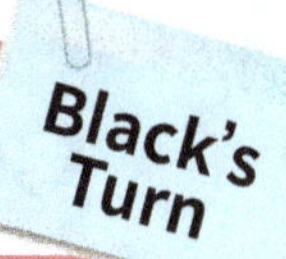

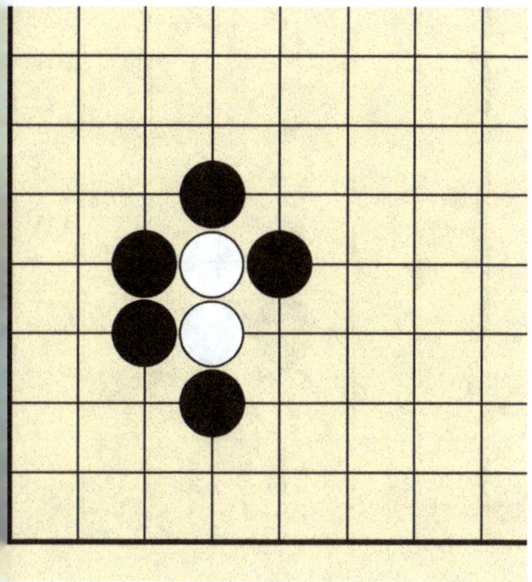

11

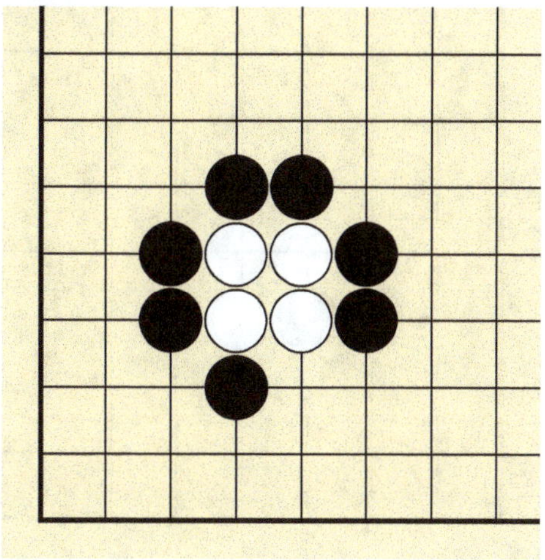

12

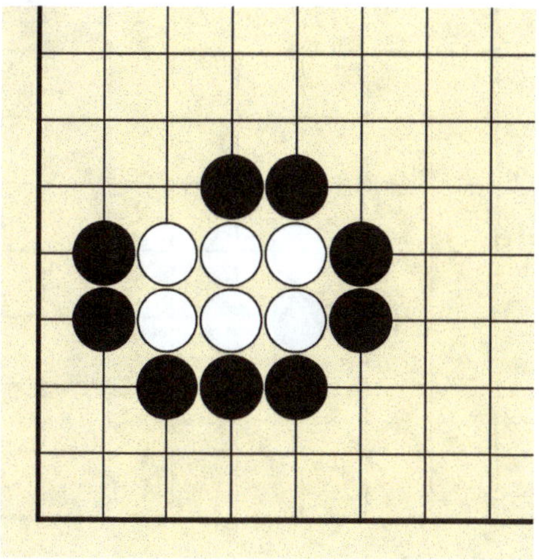

3

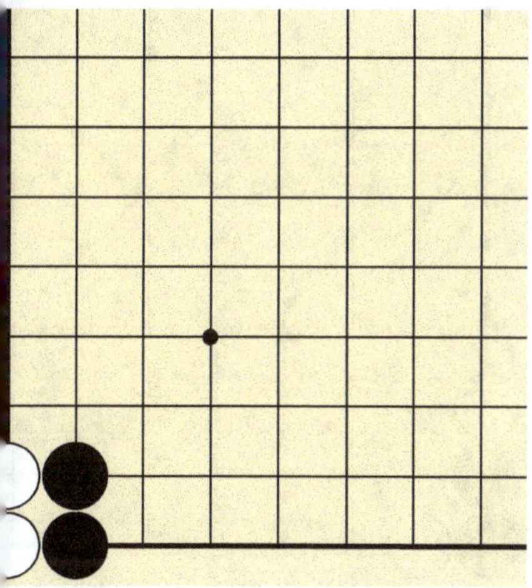

14

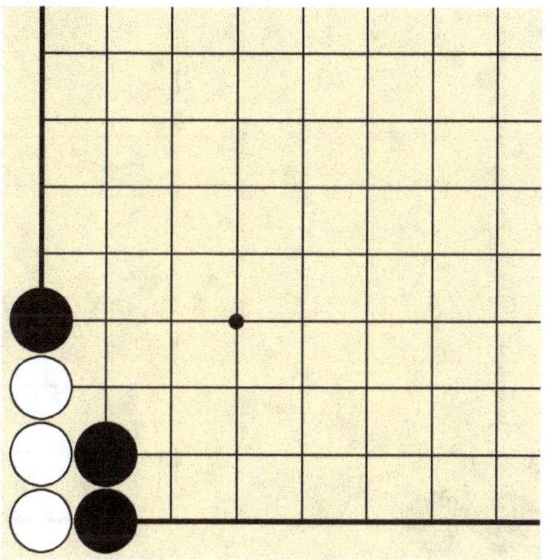

15

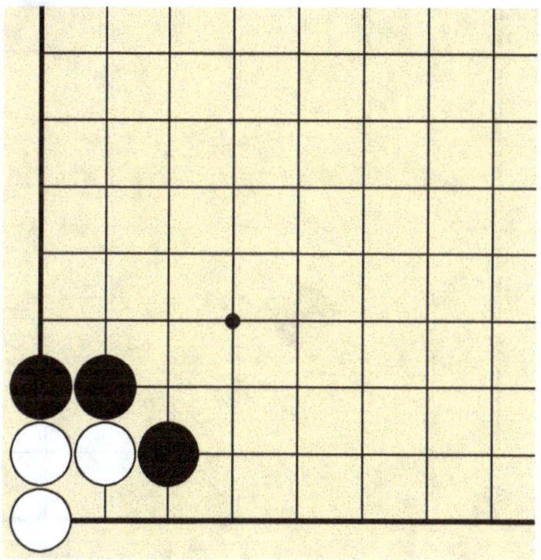

6

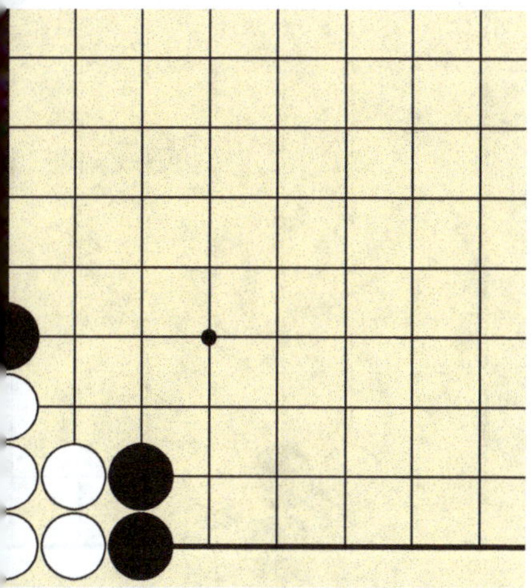

17

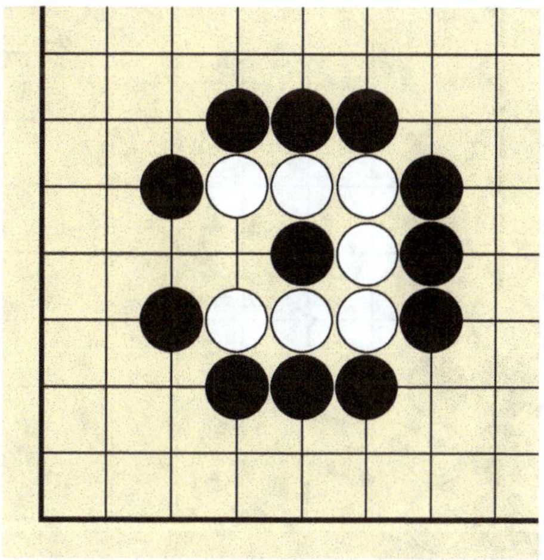

18

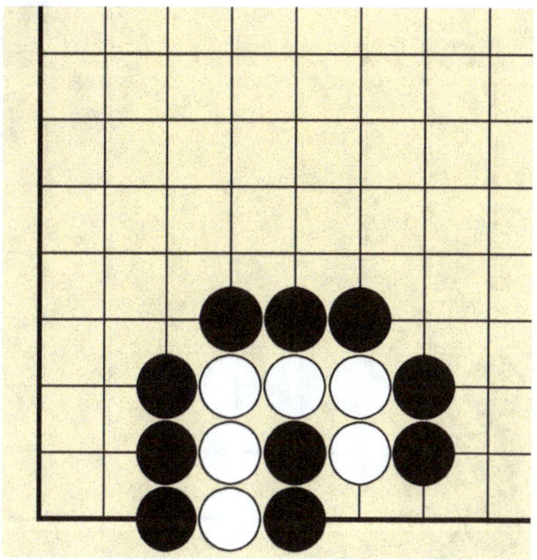

1 Capturing Game I _ 3 Saving

Black's Turn

? Save the black stones.

01

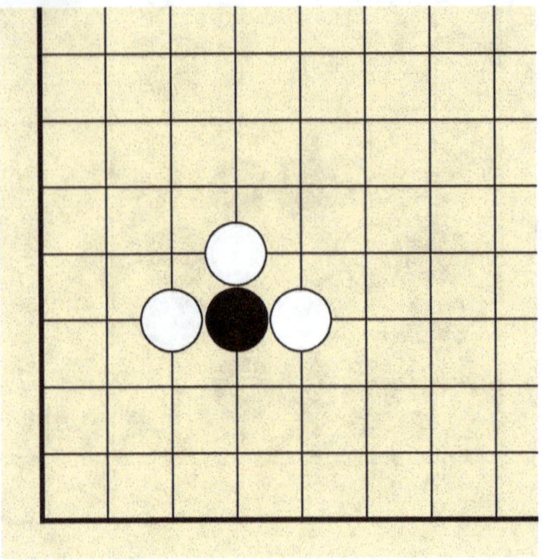

02

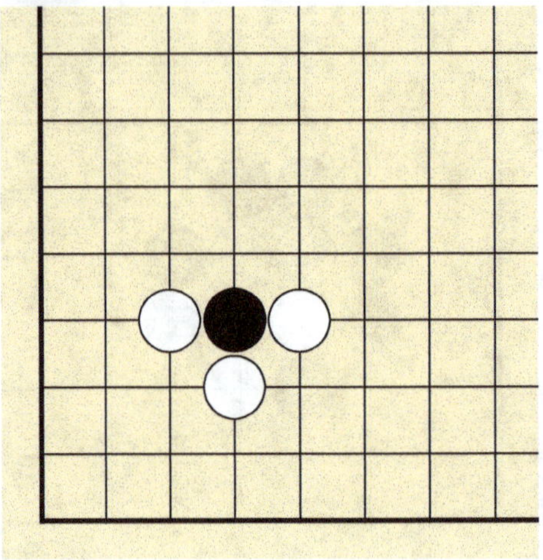

03

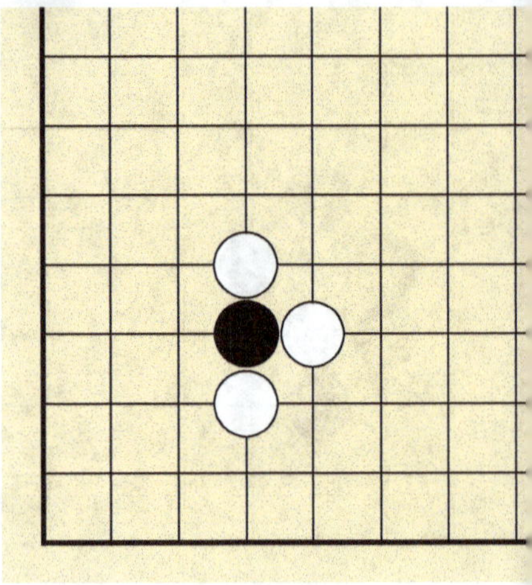

04

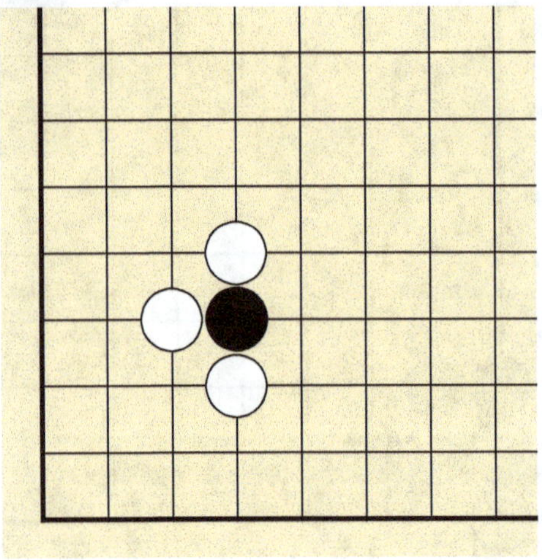

05

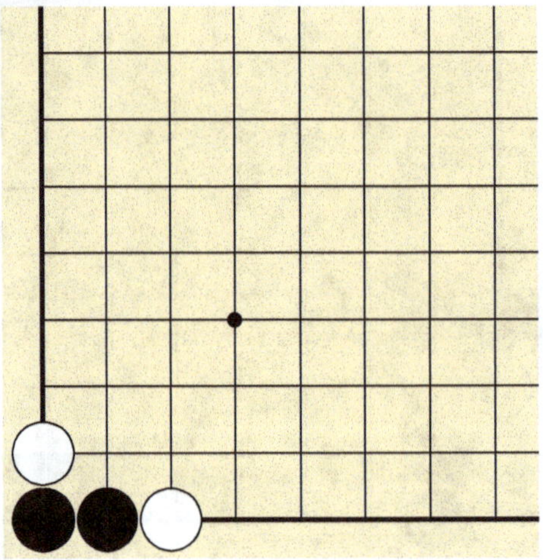

06

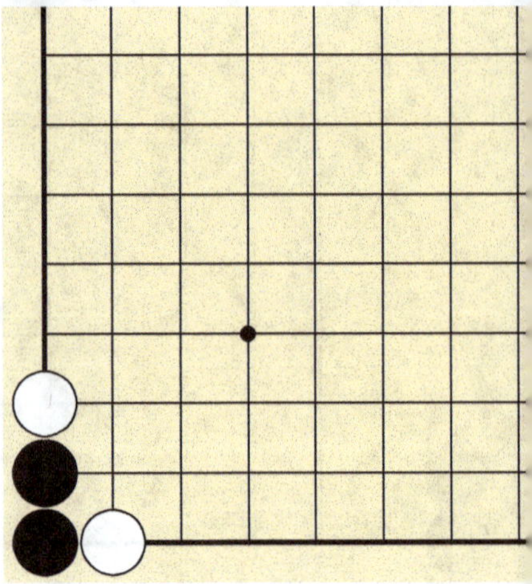

07

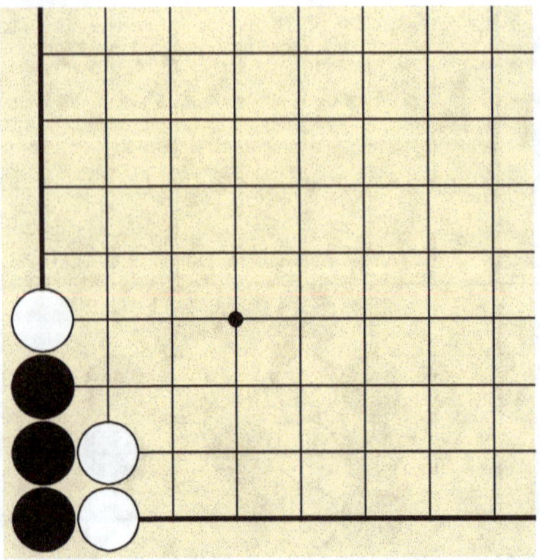

08

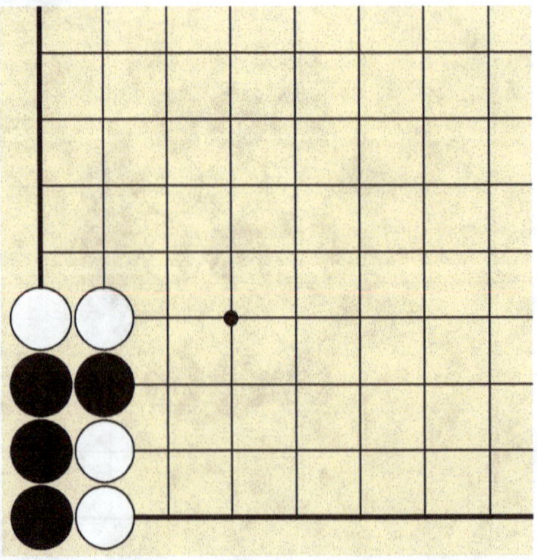

09

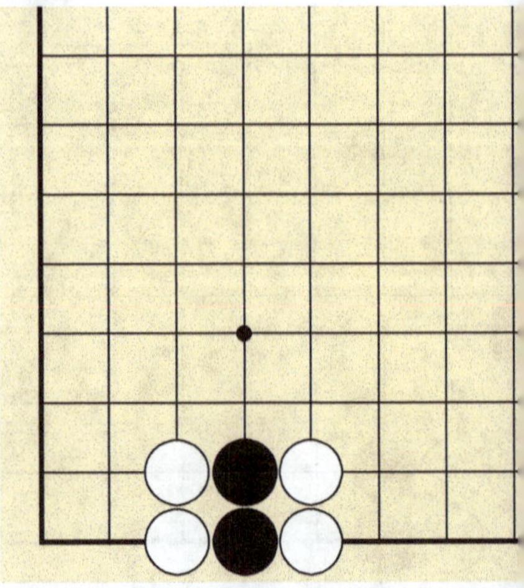

1 Capturing Game I _ 3 Saving

Black's Turn

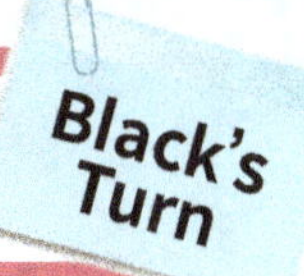

? Save the black stones.

10

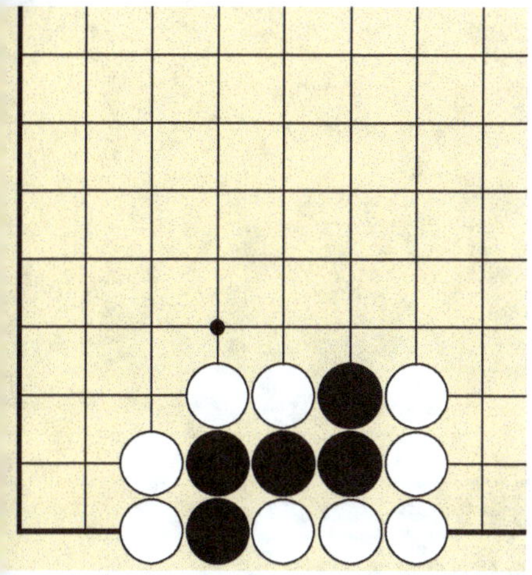

11

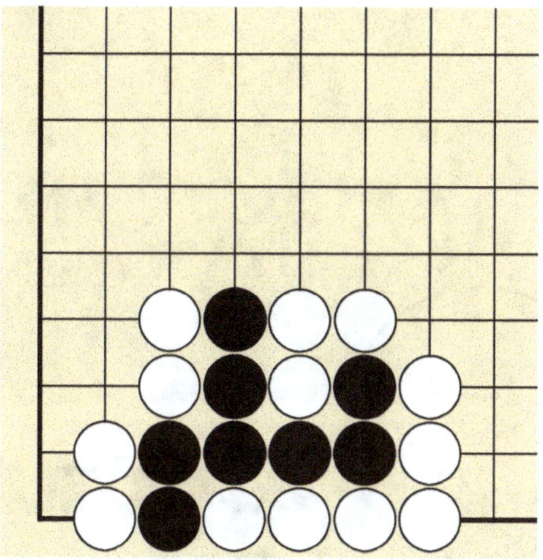

12

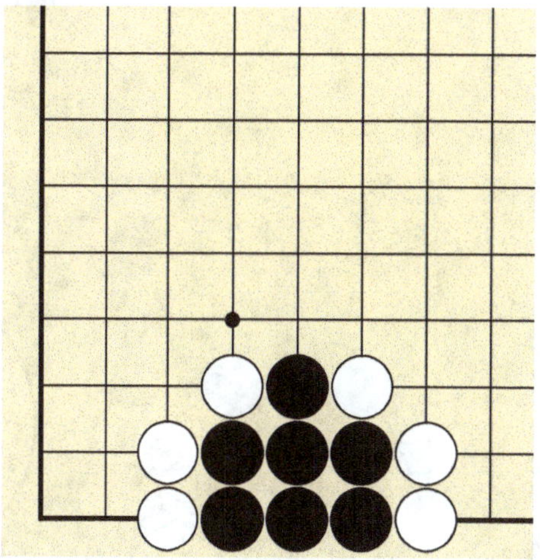

13

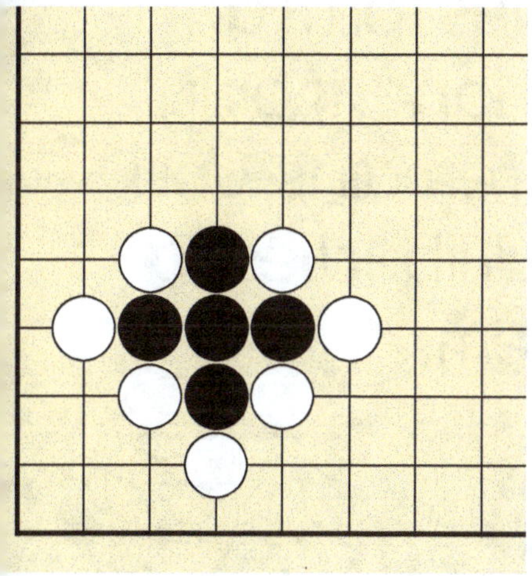

14

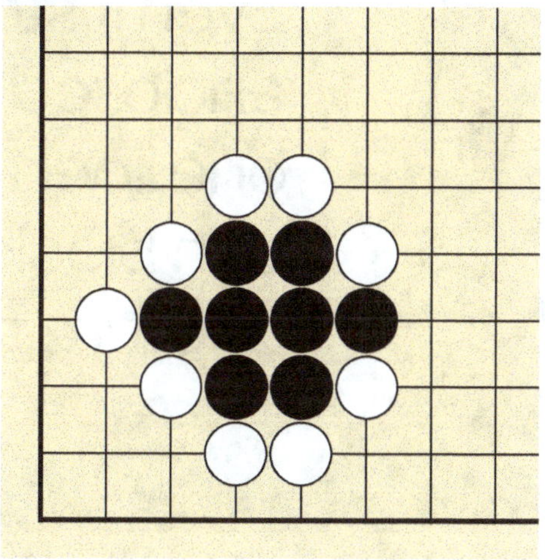

15

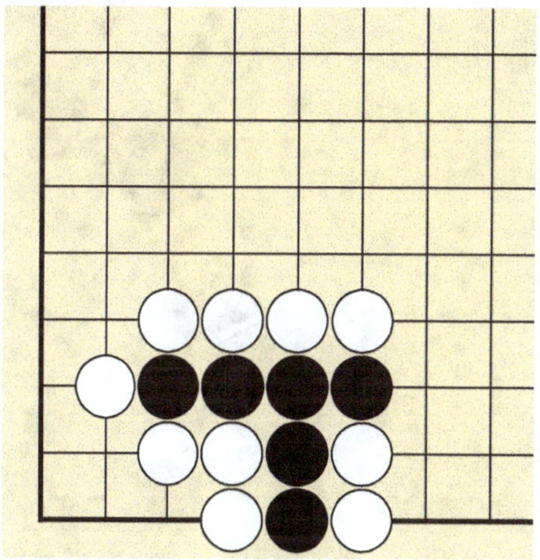

16

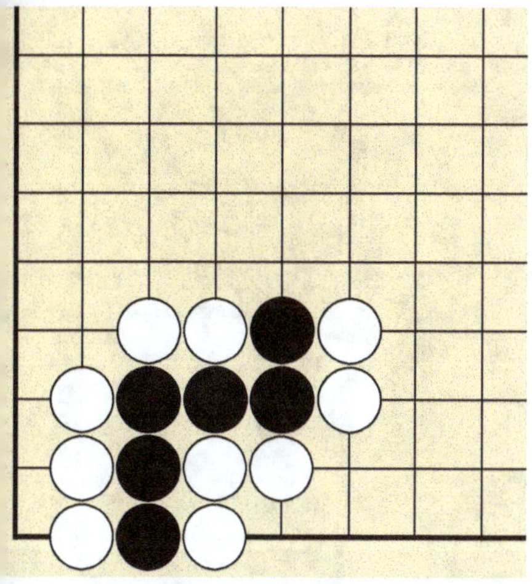

17

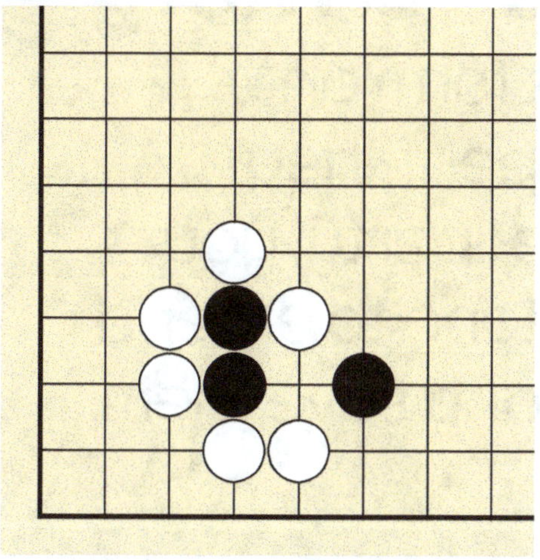

18

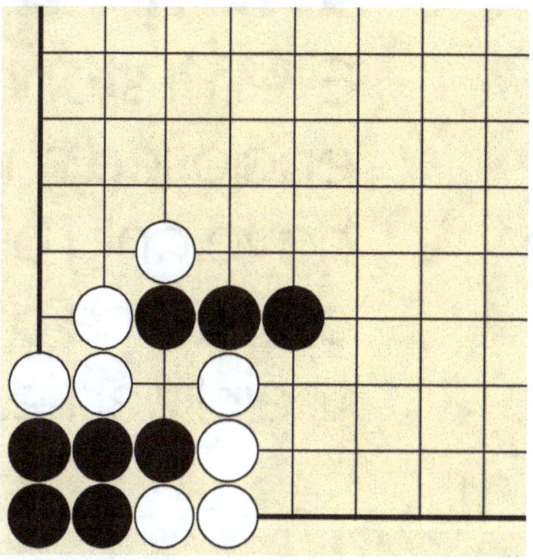

Capturing Game II

Capturing Stones Within the Territory

Even if stones form an enclosed shape, if only one liberty remains, you can block all liberties to capture them.

Saving Stones Within the Territory

Even if stones form an enclosed shape, if they have only one liberty, you can place a stone to extend their liberties and save them.

🐺 Capturing Stones Within the Territory

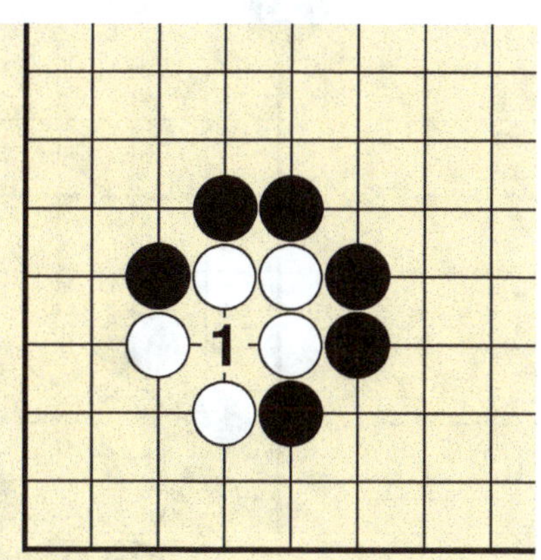

01 White stones have one liberty.

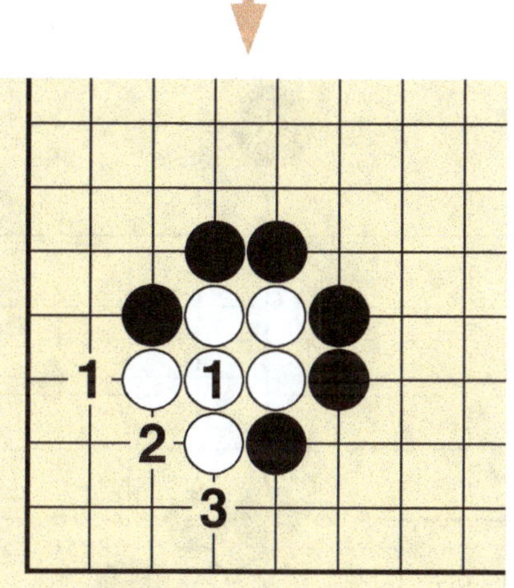

02 If a white player places a stone (White 1) first, then white stones gain more liberties.

03 Conversely if a black player place a black stone (Black 1) first, then white stones are captured.

🐺 Saving Stones Within the Territory

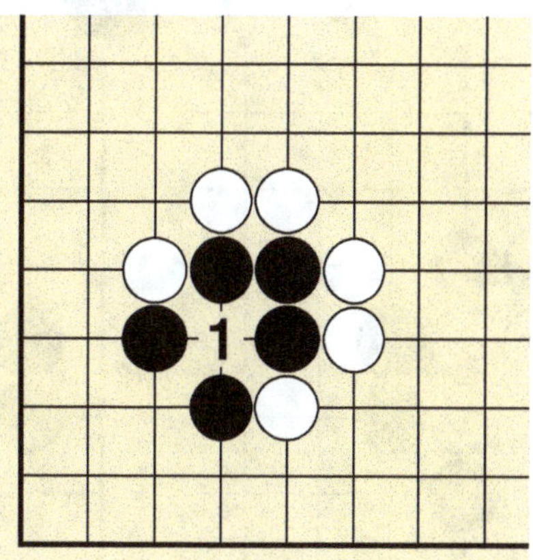

01 Black stones have one liberty.

02 If white moves first and blocks the liberty of the black stones, it will be captured.

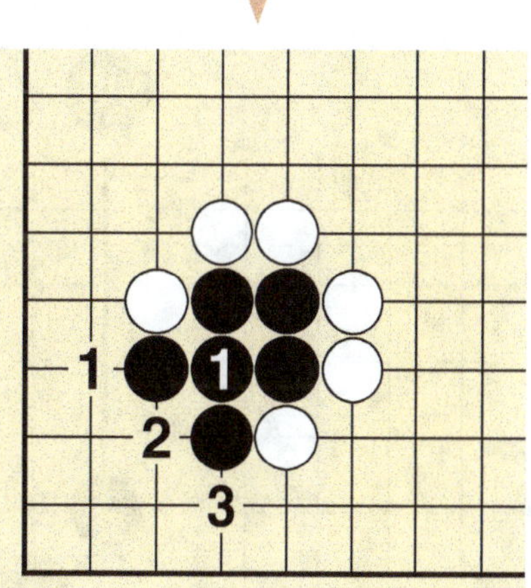

03 Place black stone (Black 1) to save the black stones.

? **Capture the white stones.**

01

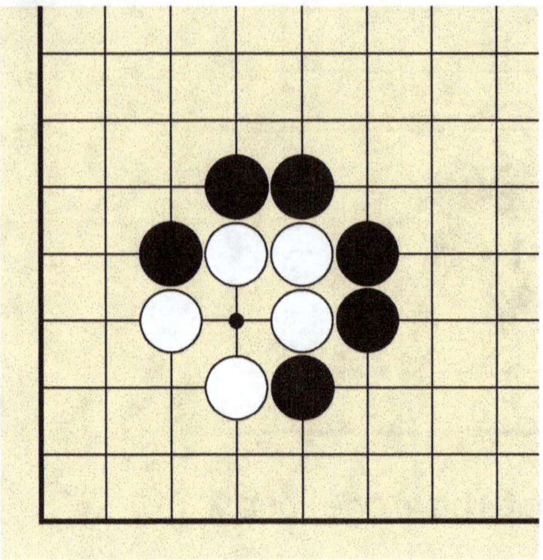

02

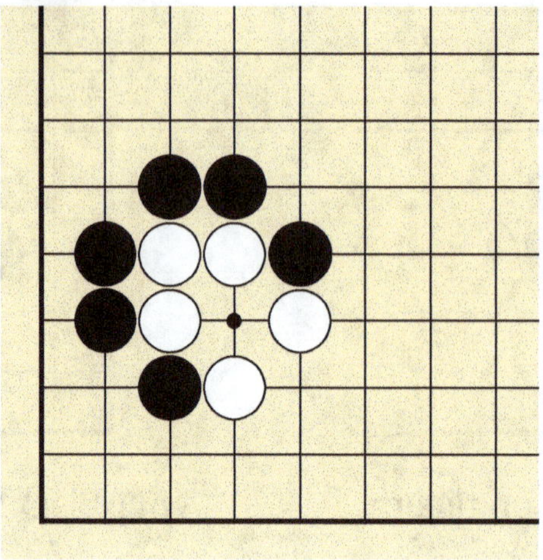

03

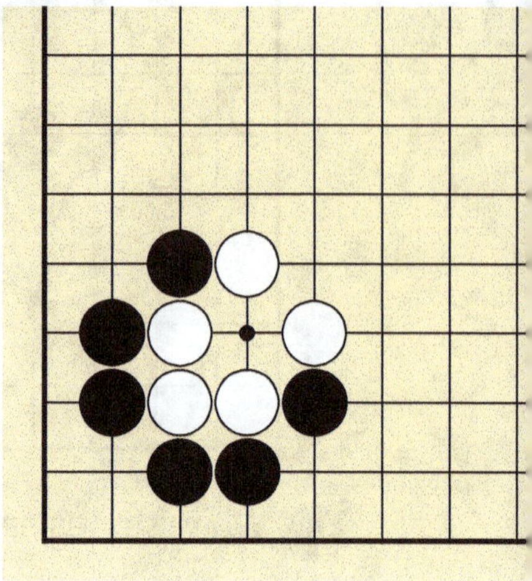

04

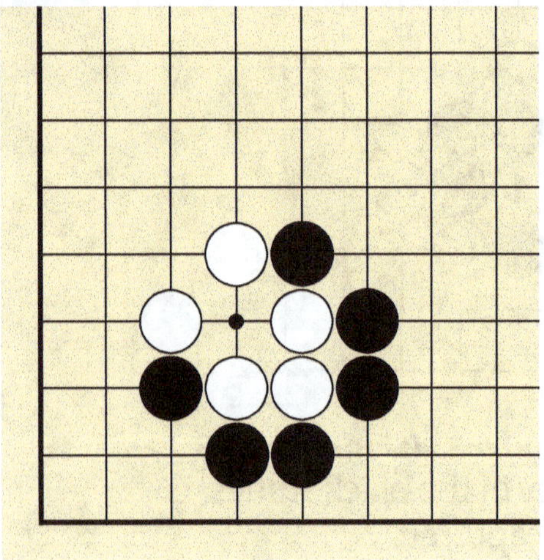

05

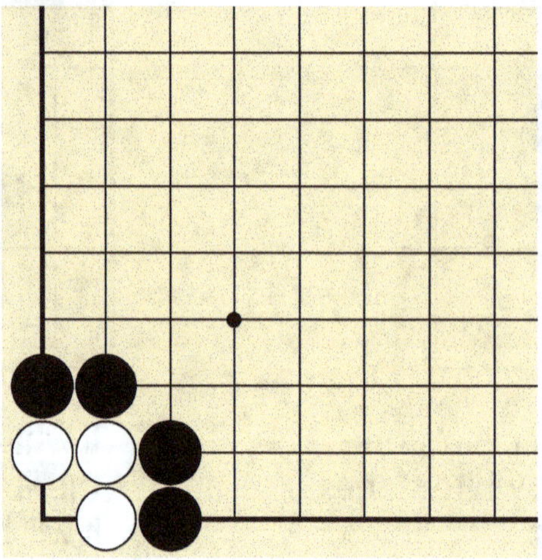

06

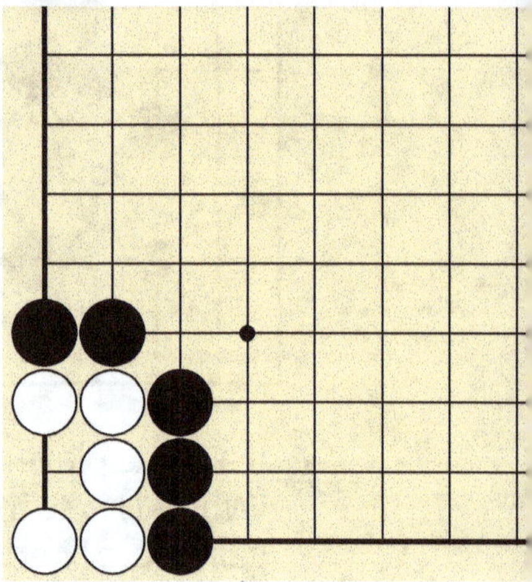

07

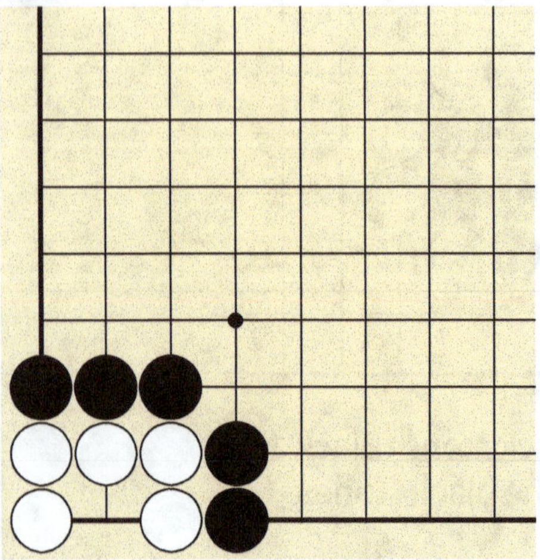

08

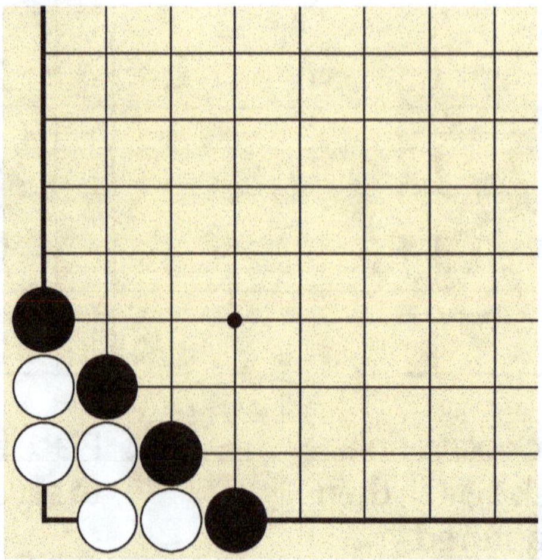

09

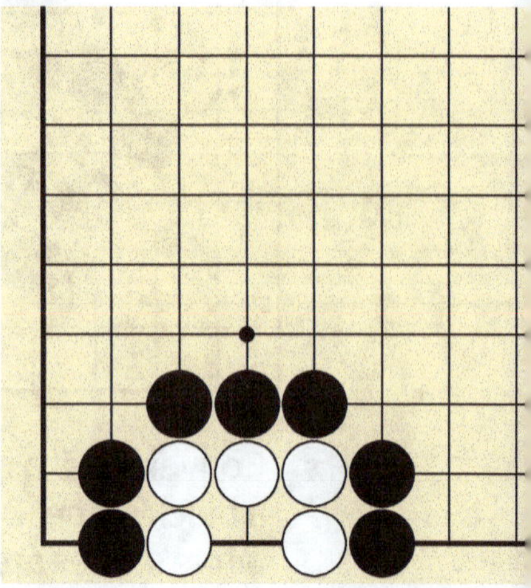

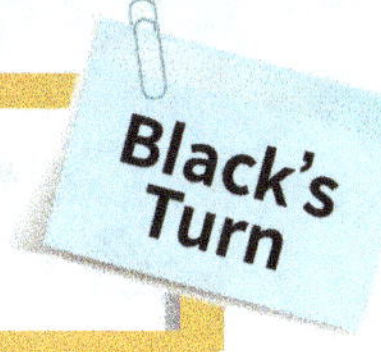

2 Capturing Game II _
❶ Capturing stones Within the Territory

Black's Turn

? Capture the white stones.

10

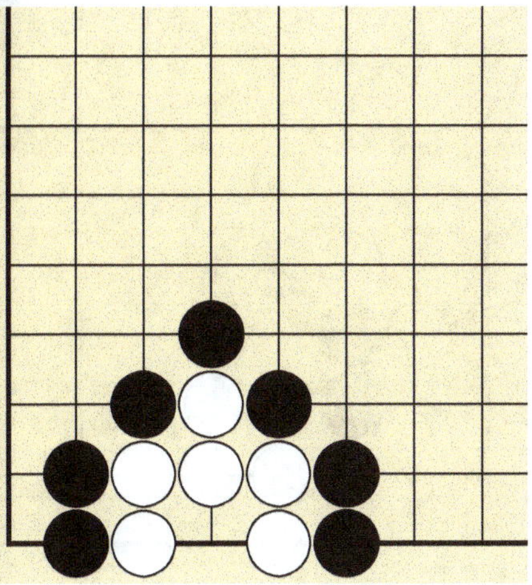

11

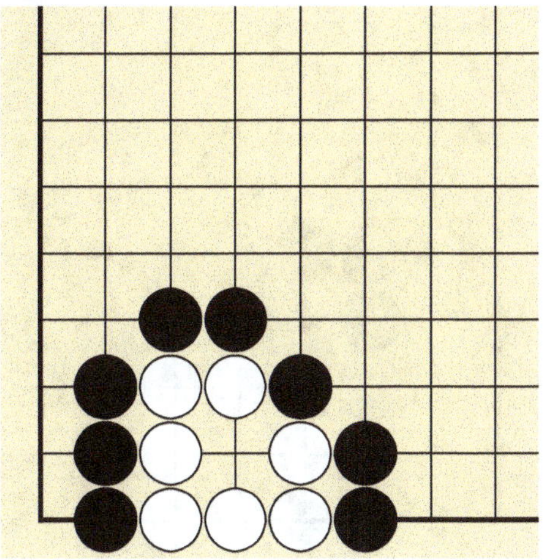

12

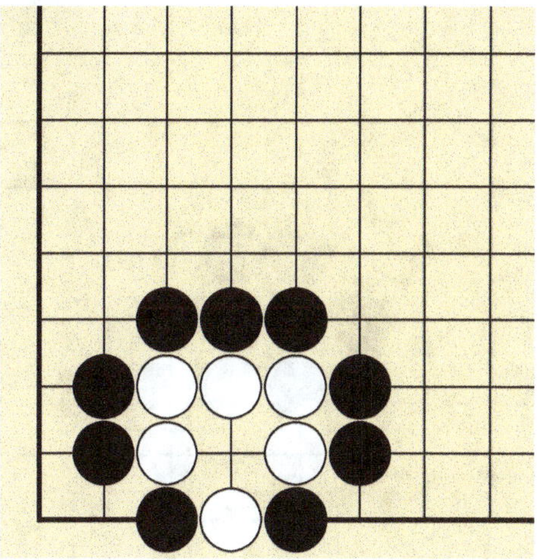

13

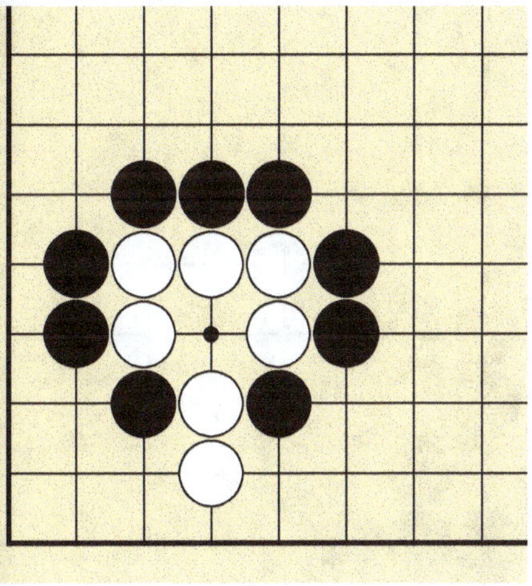

14

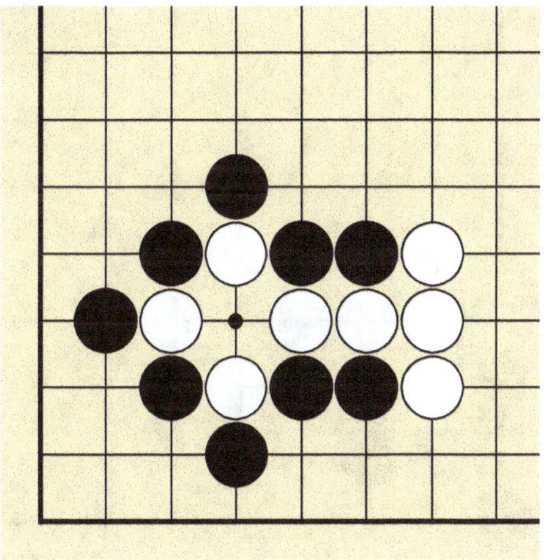

15

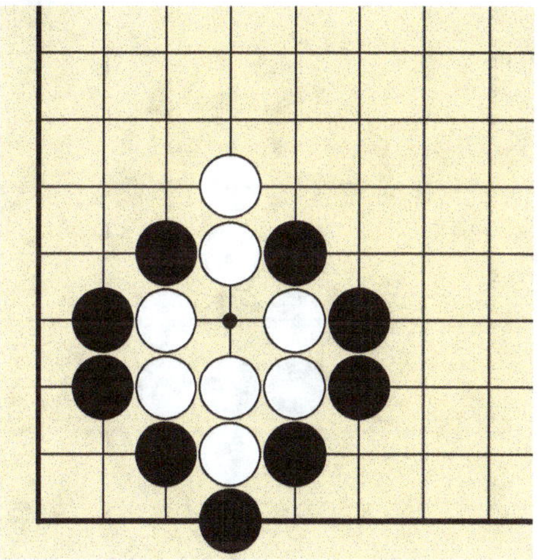

16

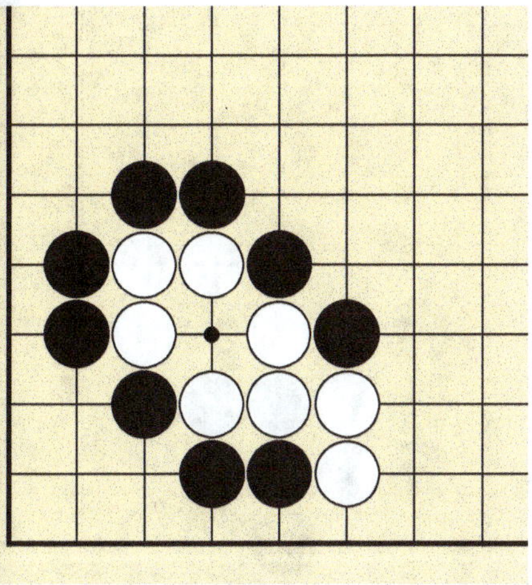

17

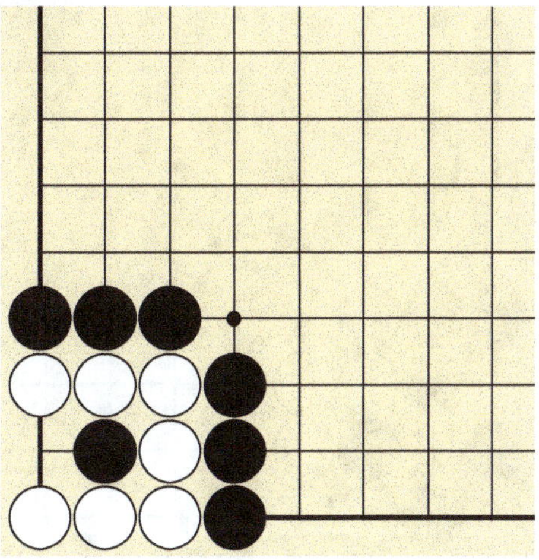

18

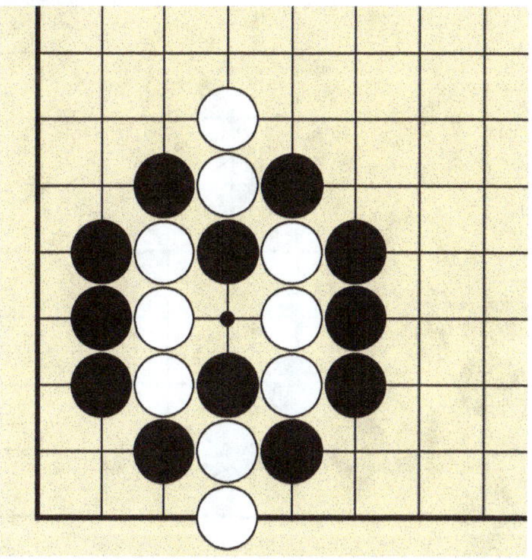

? **Save the black stones.**

01

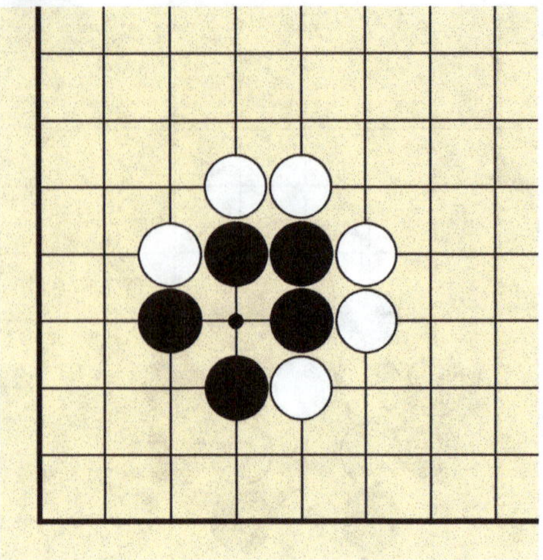

02

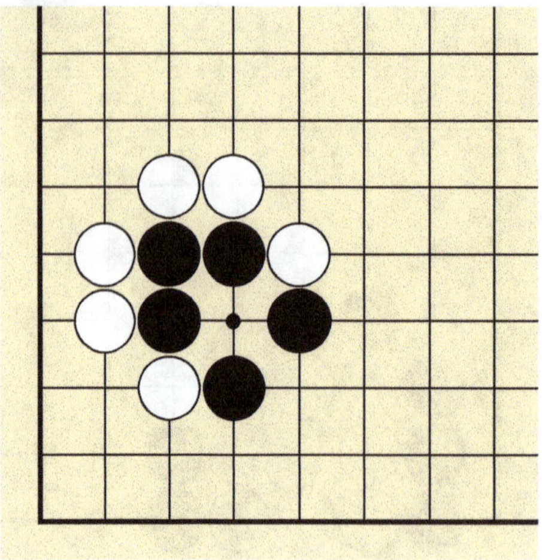

03

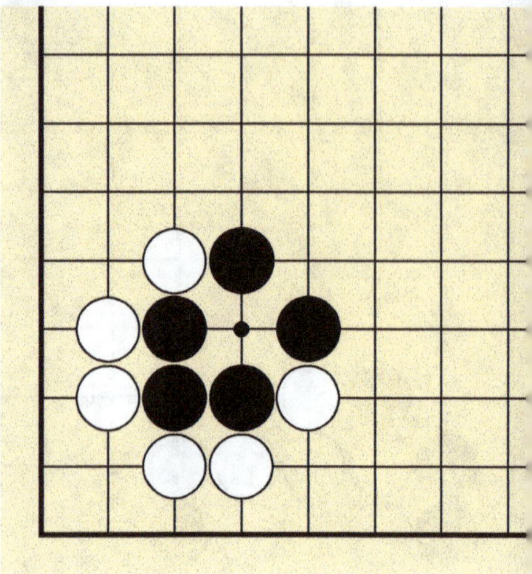

04

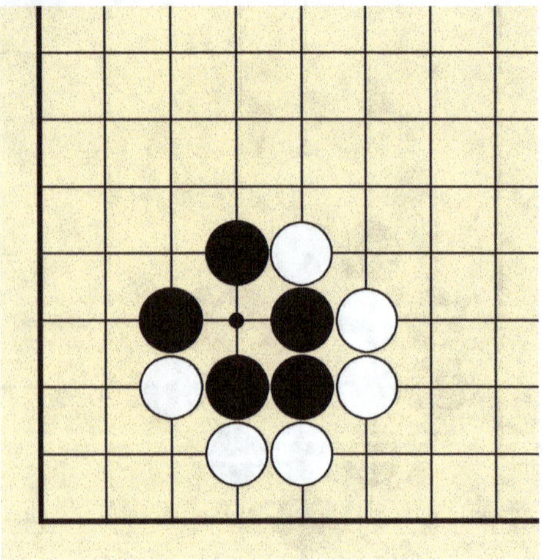

05

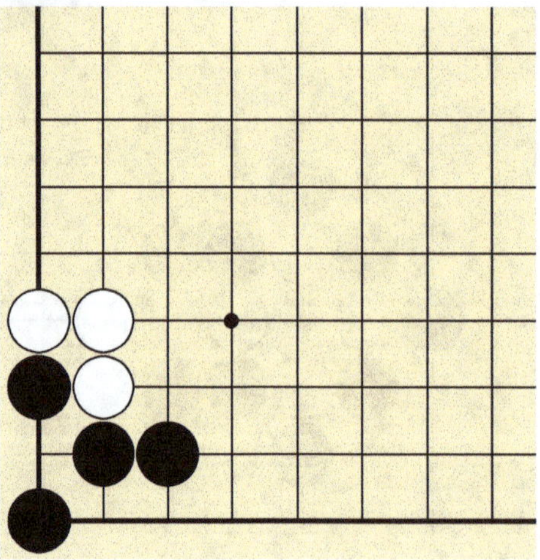

06

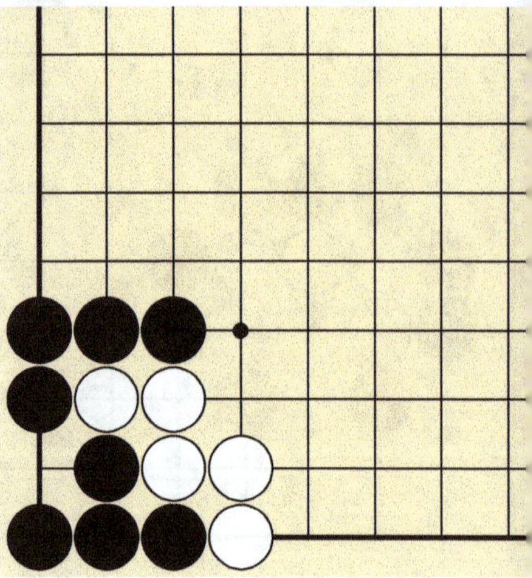

07

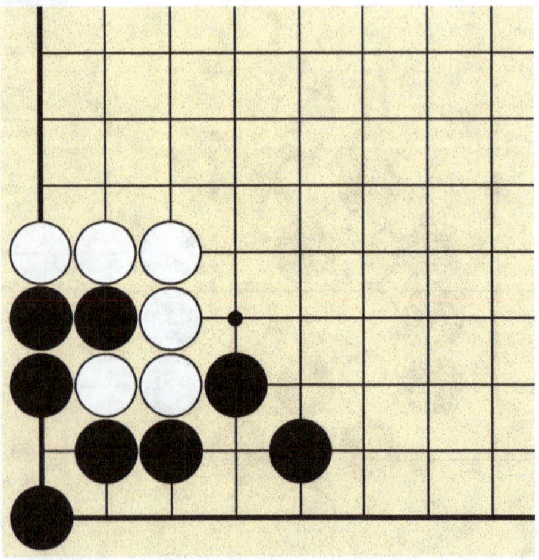

08

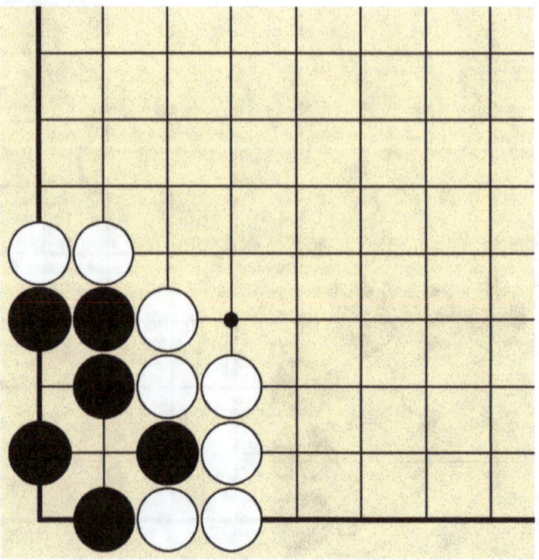

09

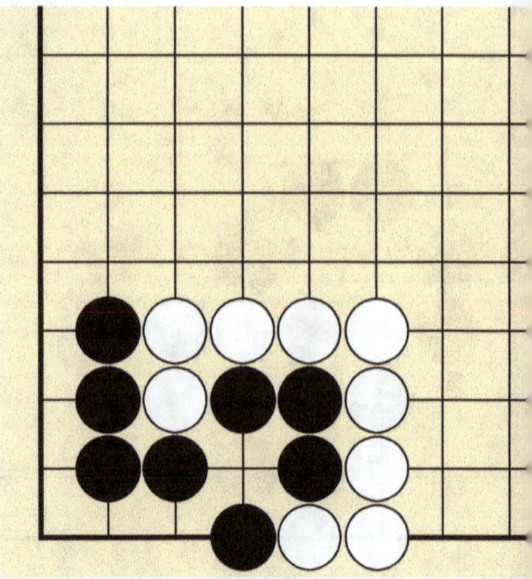

? **Save the black stones.**

10

11

12

13

14

15

16

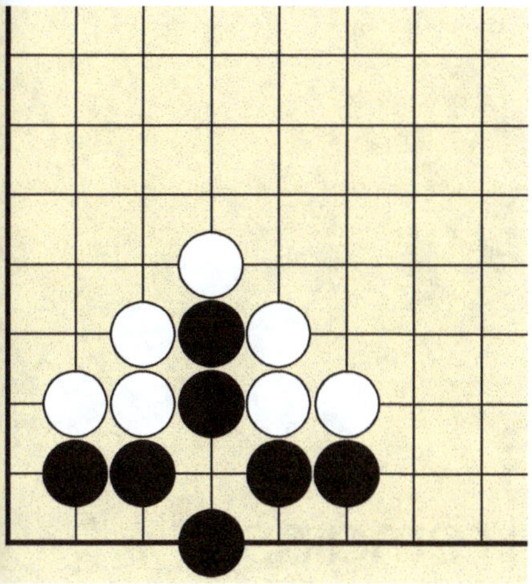

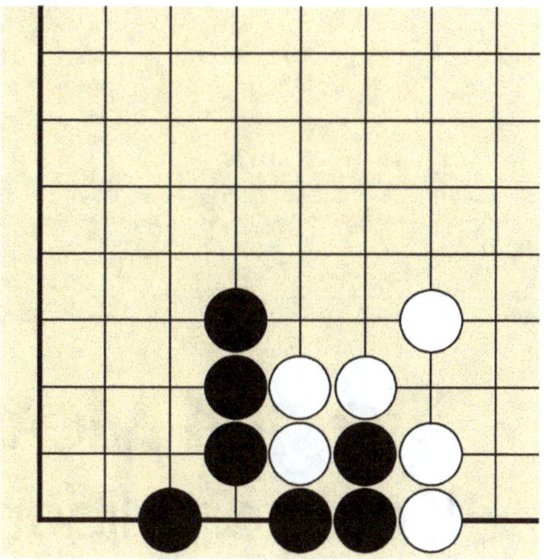

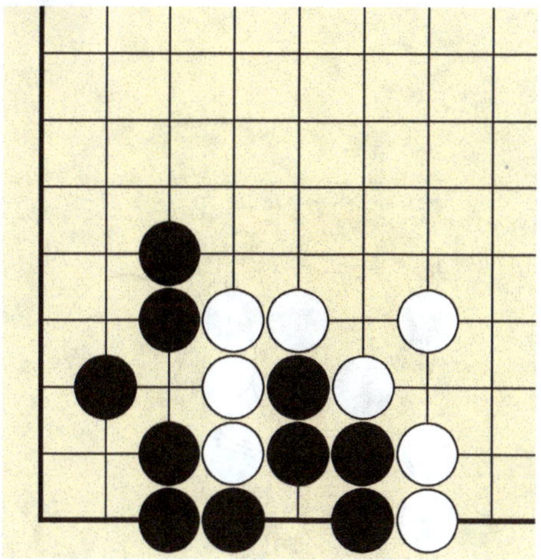

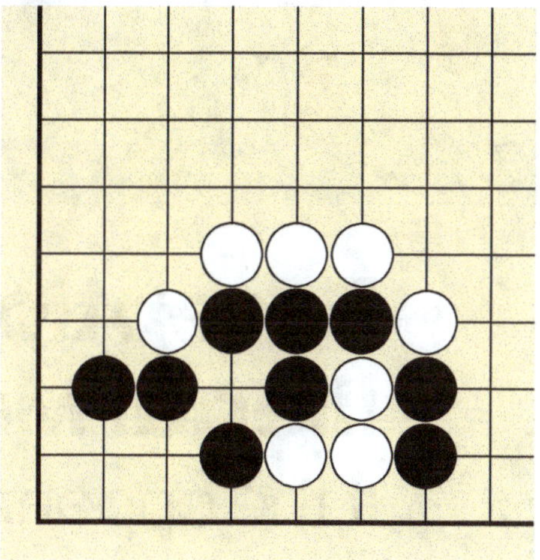

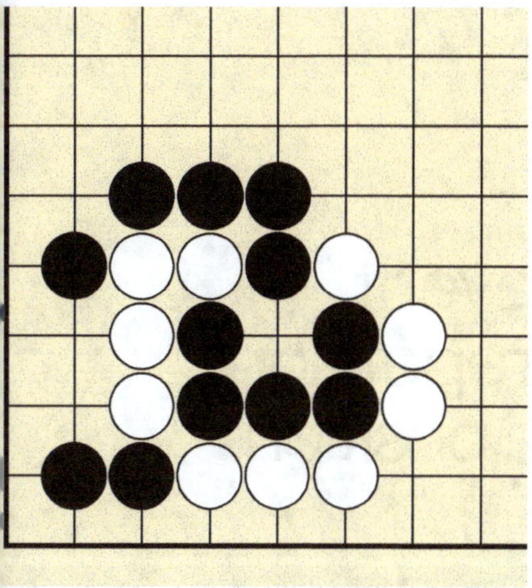

17

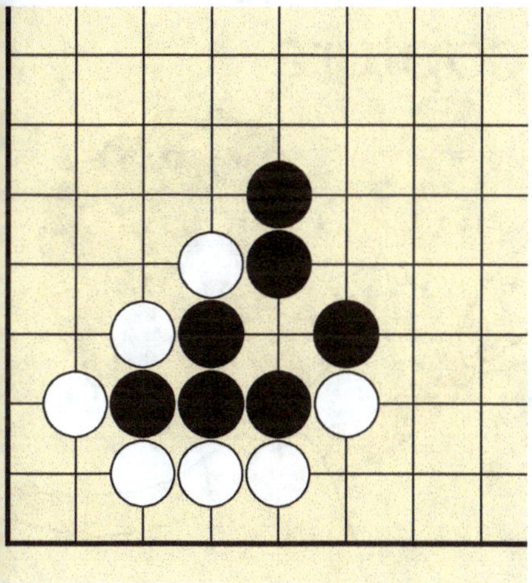

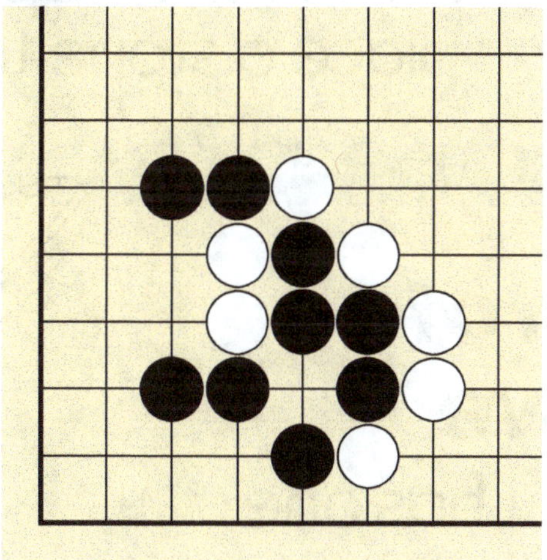

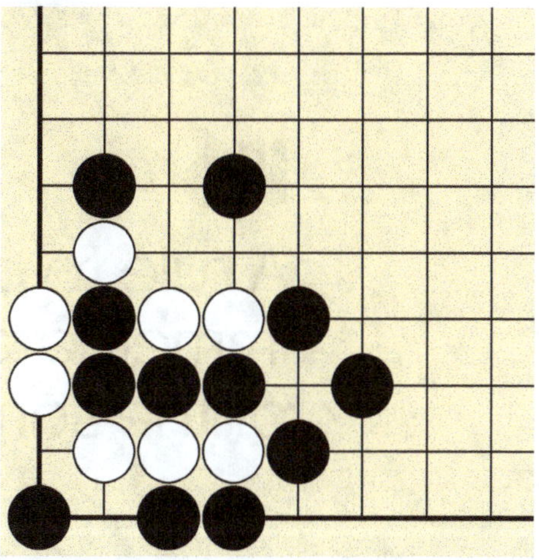

18

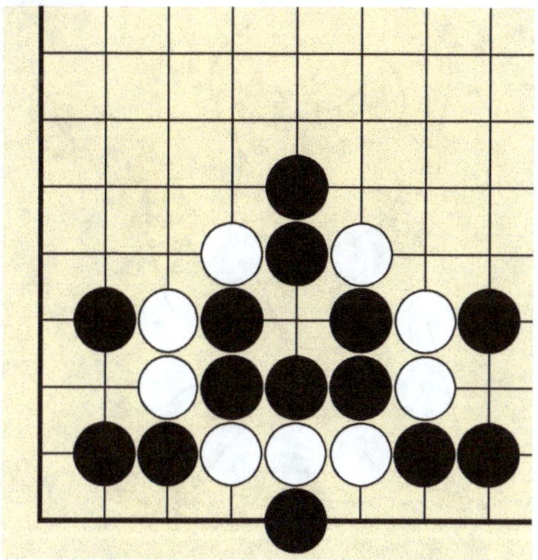

3 Must-Know Rules

Illegal Move

If only one liberty remains, you are not allowed to place your stone there; however, an opponent can place a stone to capture.

Exception of Illegal Move

If the opponent has one liberty, you can place your stone to capture it.

Ko

A rule to prevent immediate repetition of the same position.

3 Must-Know Rules _

❶ Illegal Move · ❷ Exception of Illegal Move · ❸ Ko

Illegal Move

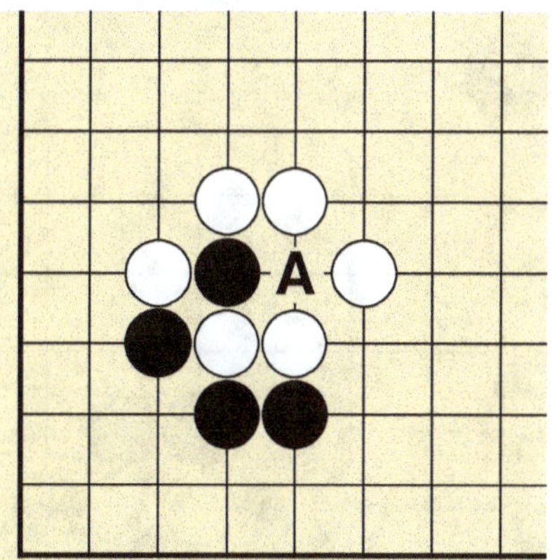

01 Do you think black can place a stone in A?

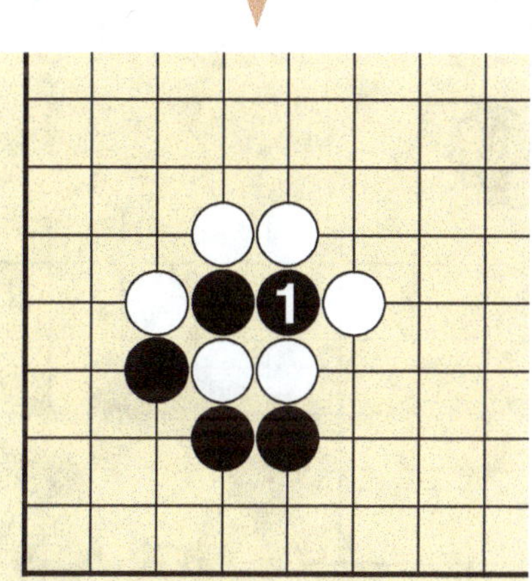

02 it is not allowed to place a stone in your last liberty.

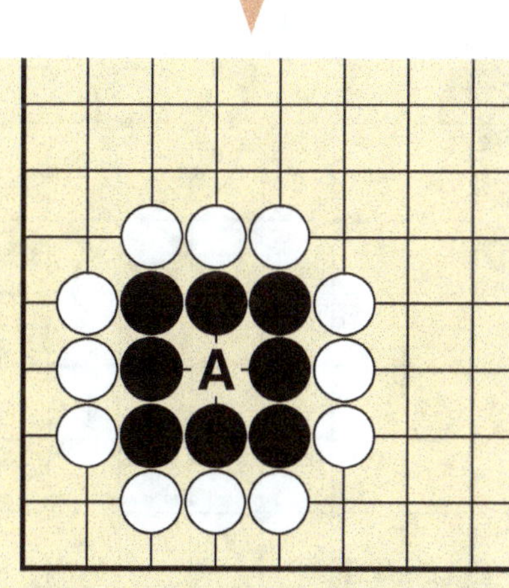

03 Placing a stone in your last liberty is called an illegal move, because you are taking your own liberty away.

Exception of Illegal Move

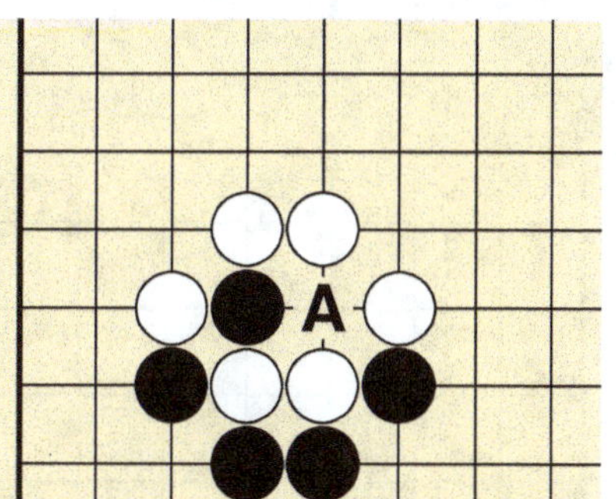

01 Can black place a stone in A?

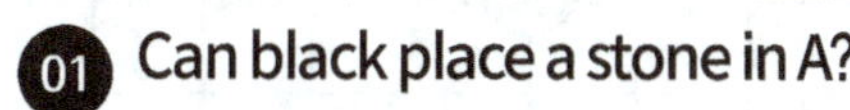

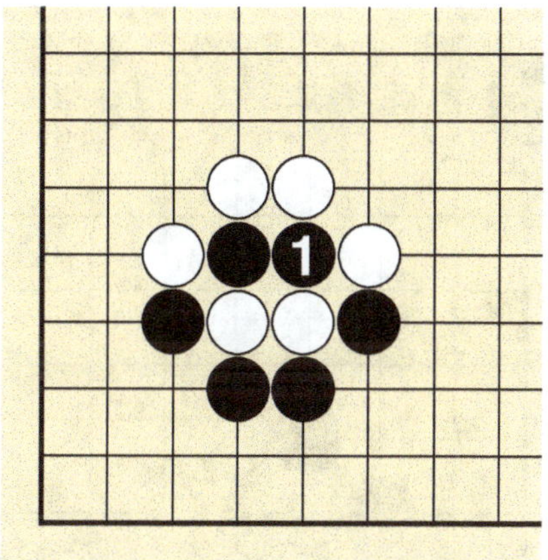

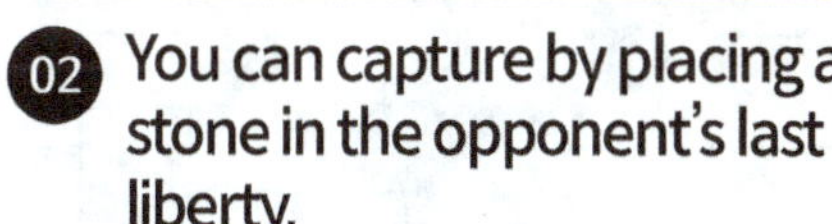

02 You can capture by placing a stone in the opponent's last liberty.

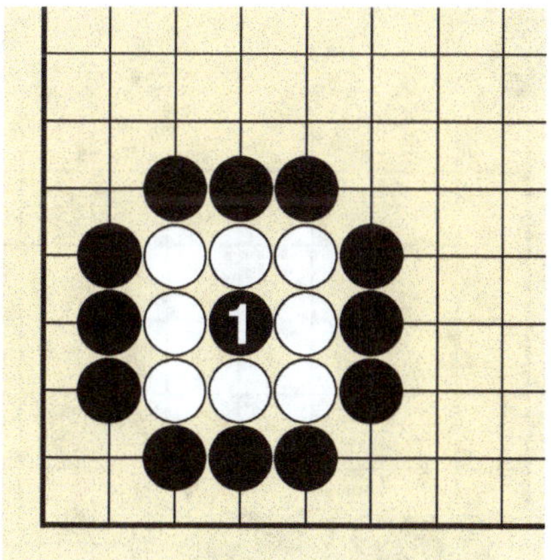

03 Capturing a stone/stones is an exception to the illegal move rule.

Ko

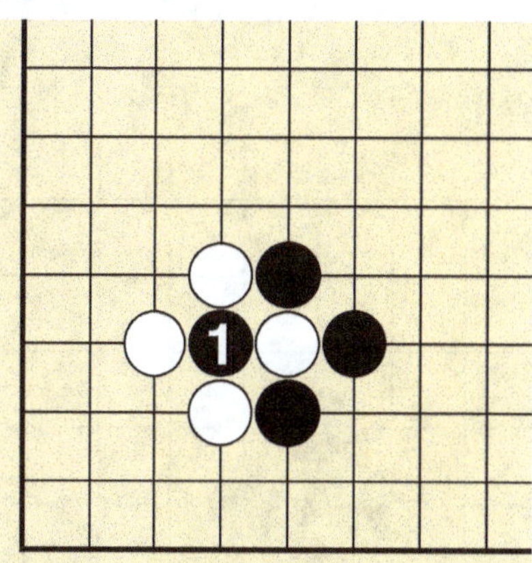

01 When the shape starts, you can capture.

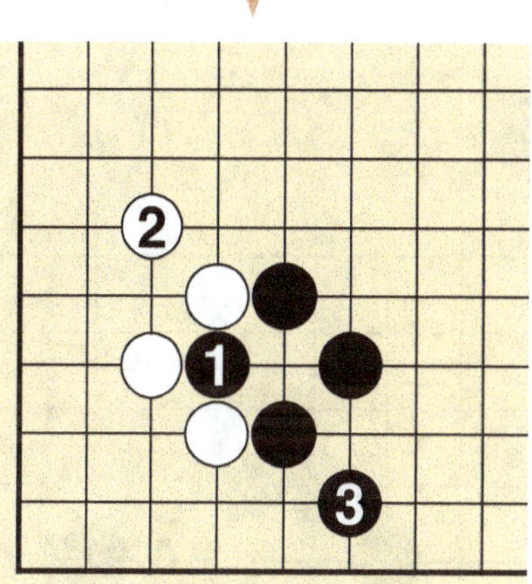

02 if the same shape repeats, the two players must place stones in other locations before capture again.

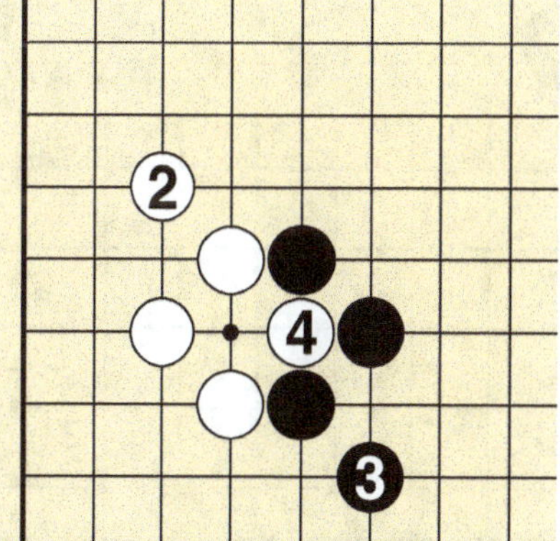

03 The rule to prevent the repetition of the same shape is "Ko."

[?] If black can place a stone in A, mark "O"; if not, mark "X."

01 (   )

02 (   )

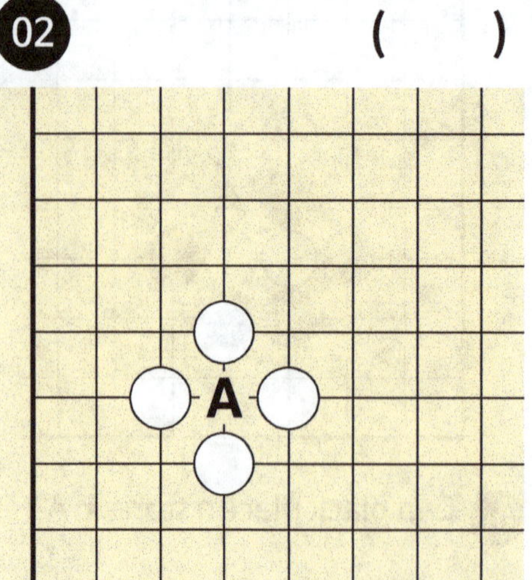

03 (   )

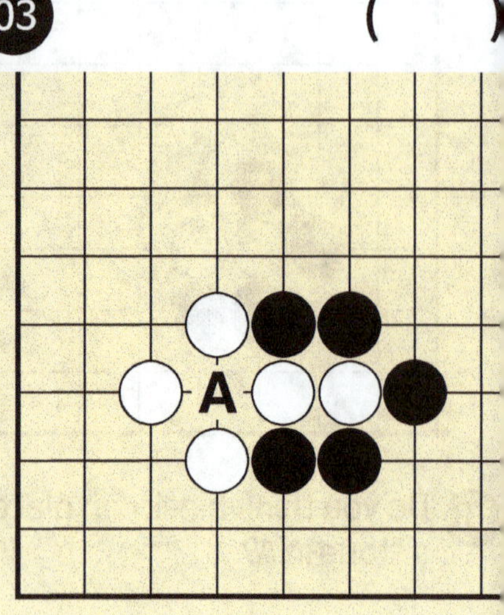

04 (   )

05 (   )

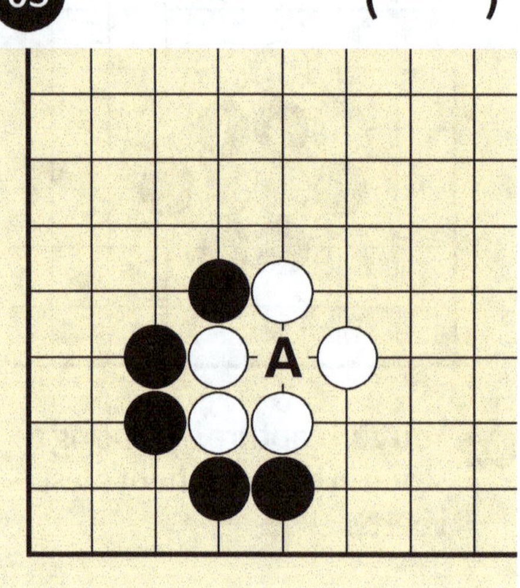

06 (   )

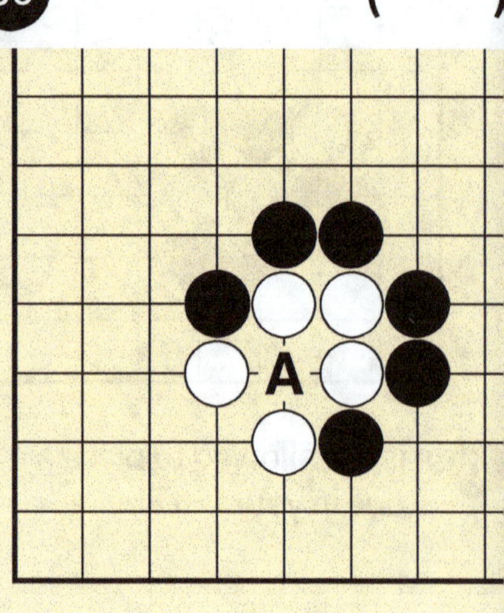

07 (   )

08 (   )

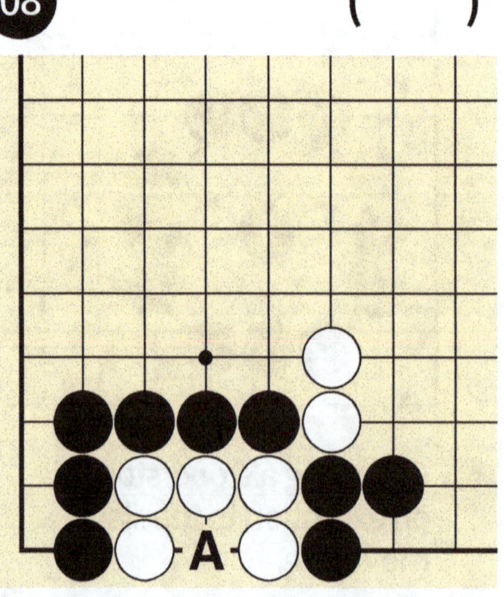

09 (   )

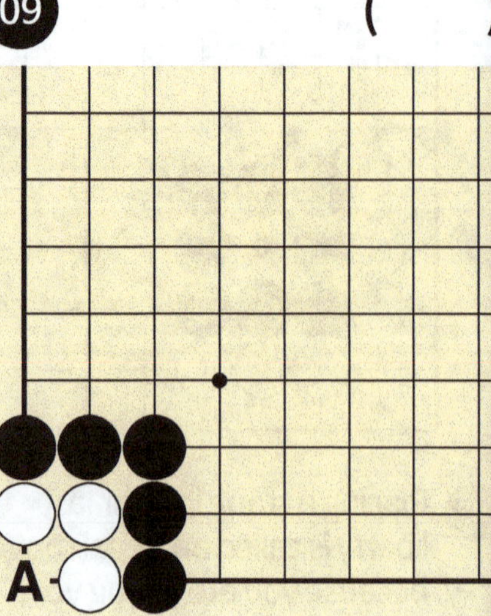

③ Must-Know Rules _
❶ Illegal Move · ❷ Exception of Illegal Move

[?] **If black can place a stone in A, mark "O"; if not, mark "X."**

10 ( )

11 ( )

12 ( )

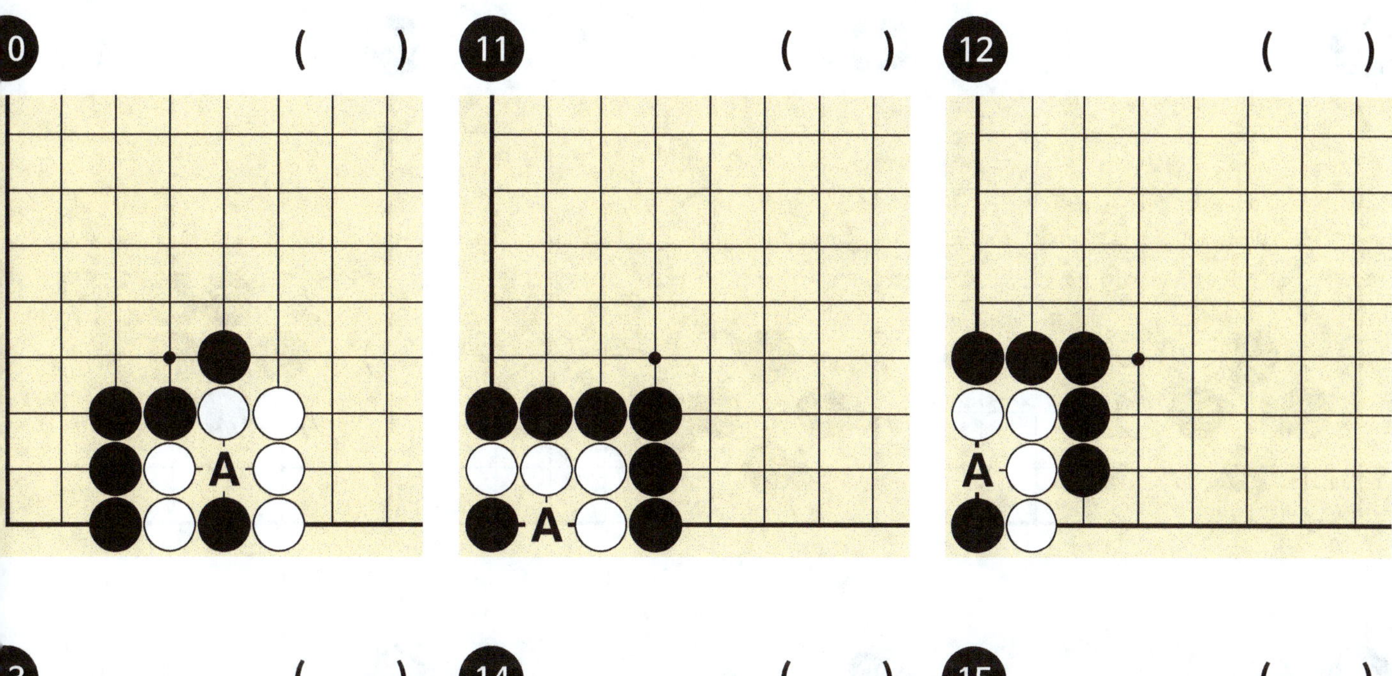

13 ( )

14 ( )

15 ( )

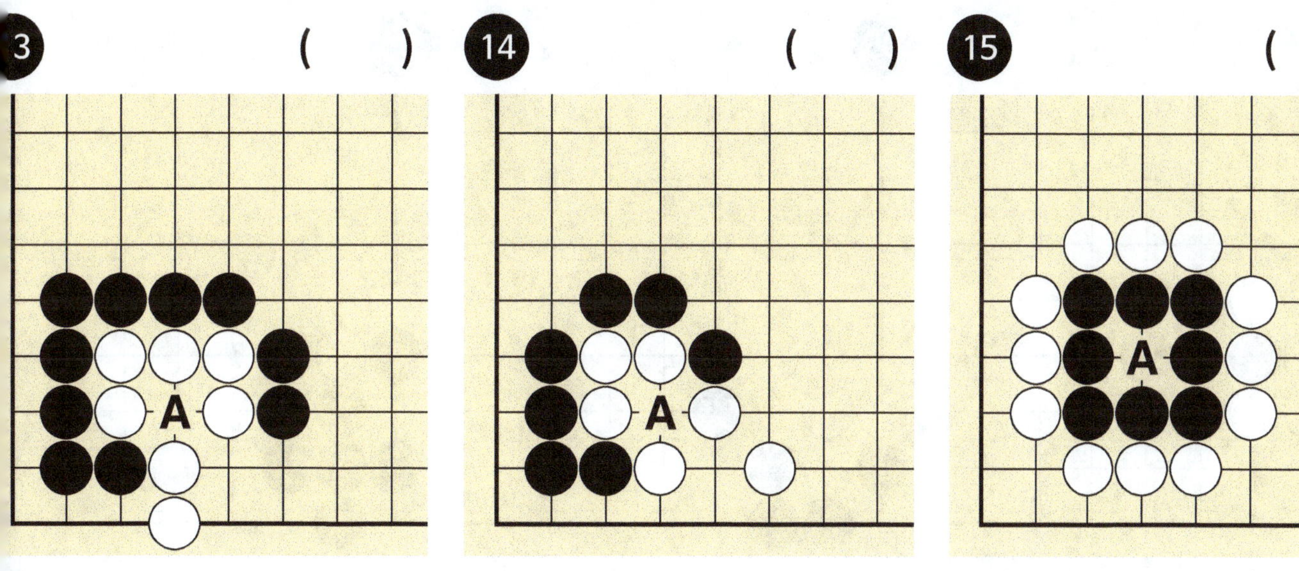

16 ( )

17 ( )

18 ( )

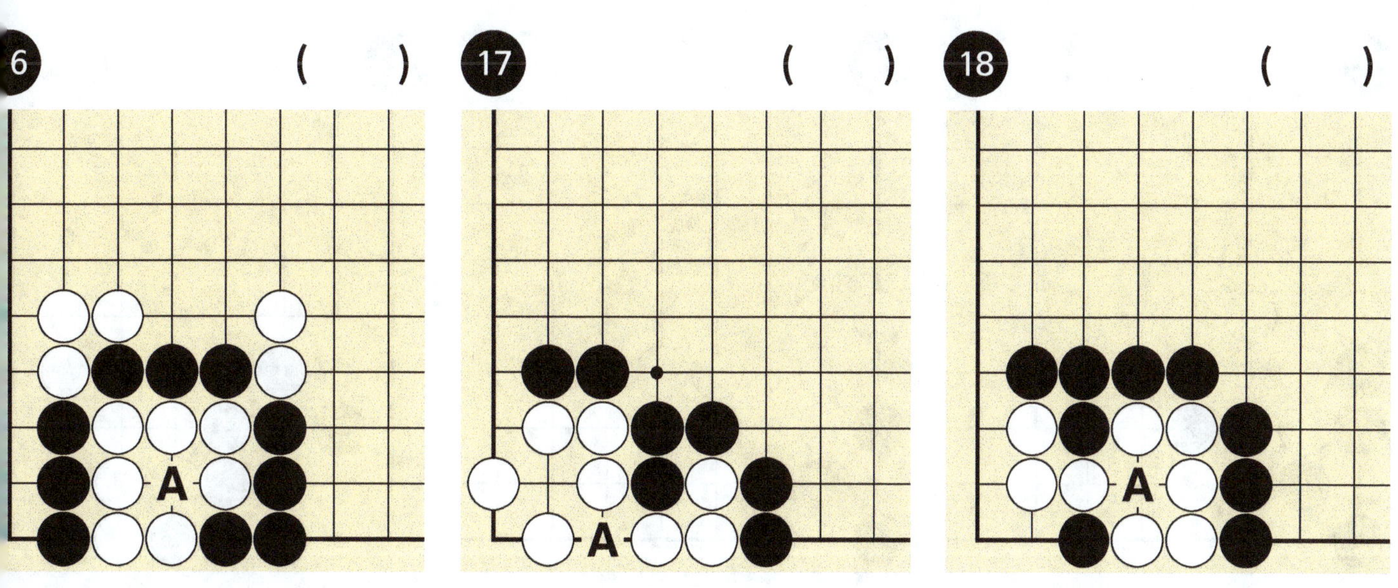

? If the shape is "Ko", mark "O"; if not, mark "X."

01 ( )

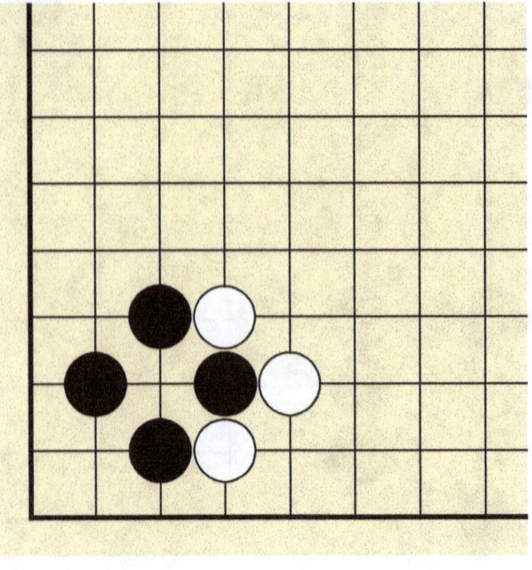

02 ( )

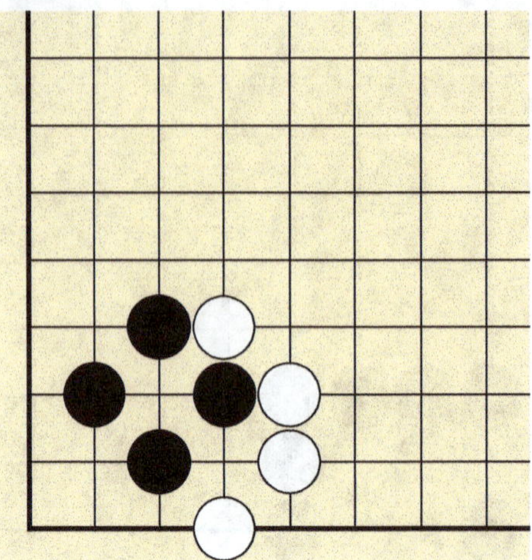

03 (

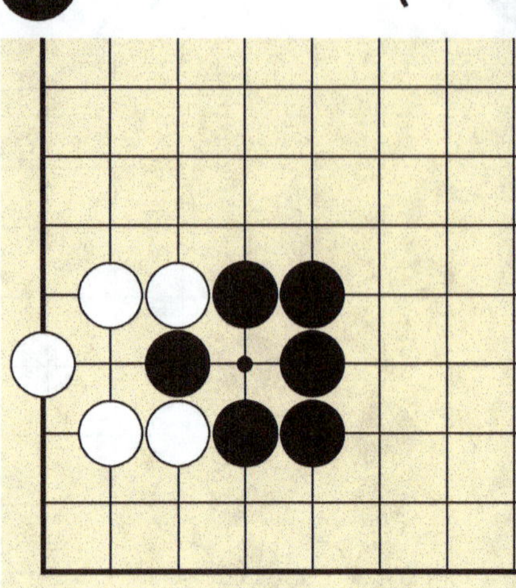

04 ( )

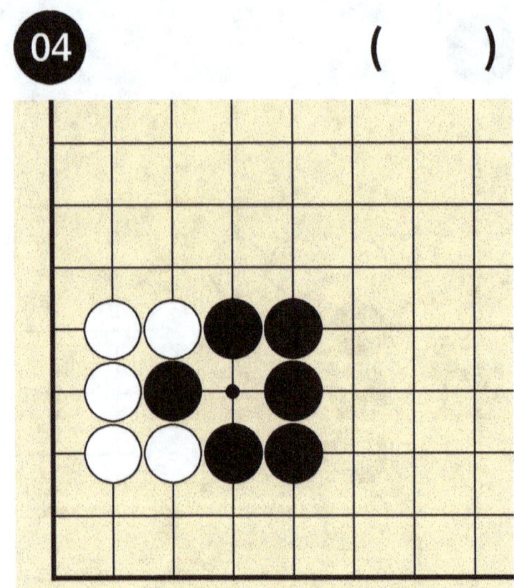

05 ( )

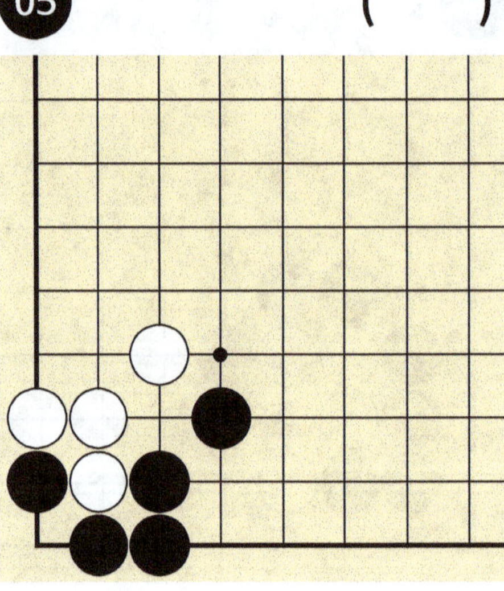

06 (

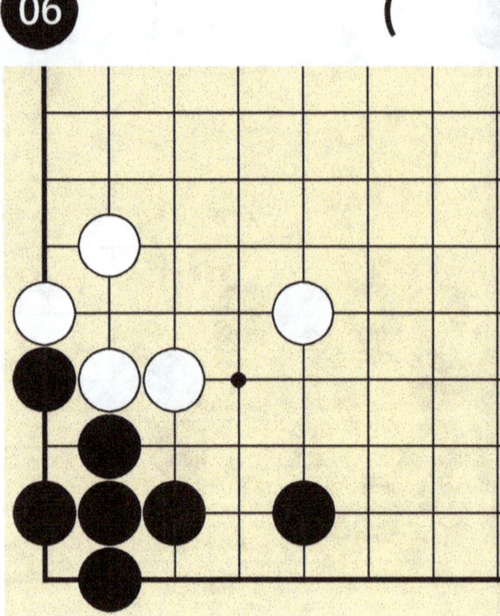

07 ( )

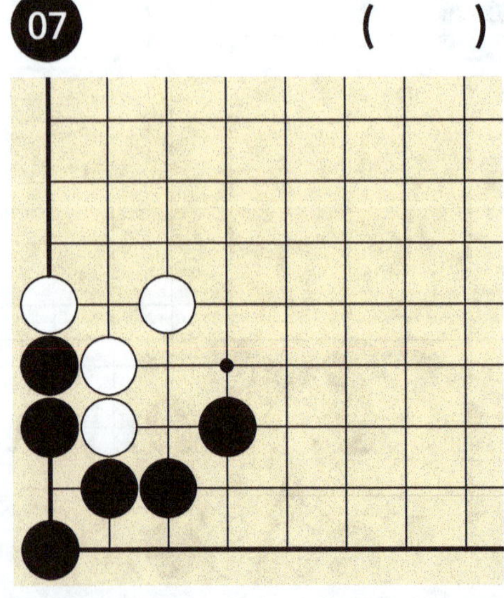

08 ( )

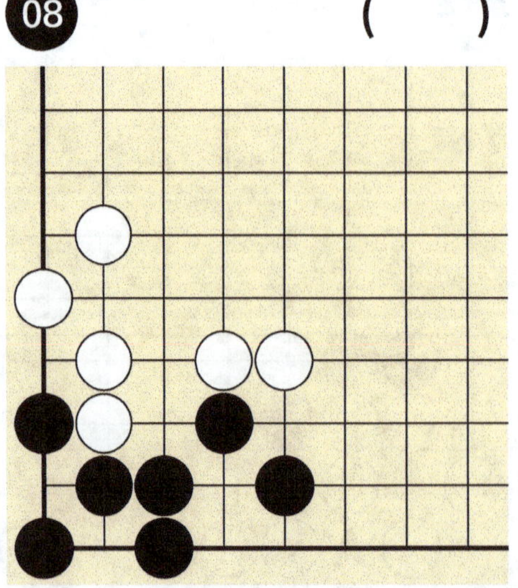

09 (

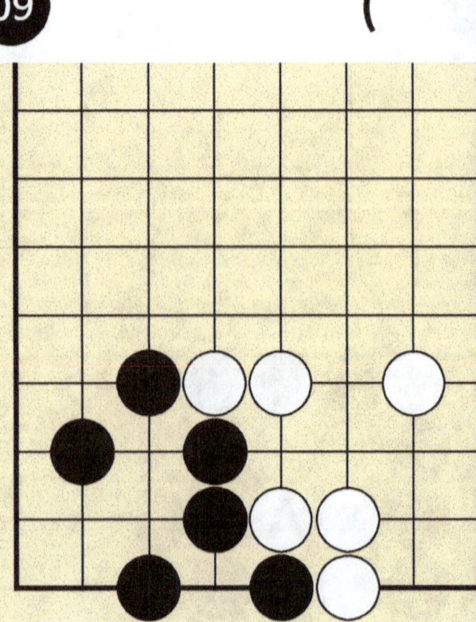

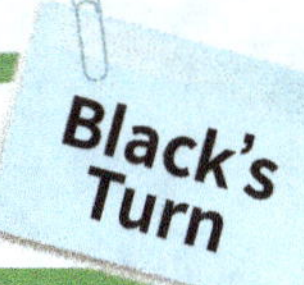

③ Must-Know Rules _ ③ Ko

Black's Turn

? Complete the shape of a "Ko."

10

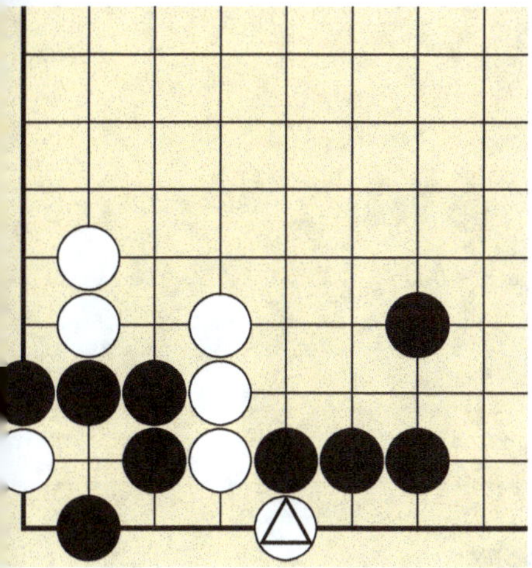

11

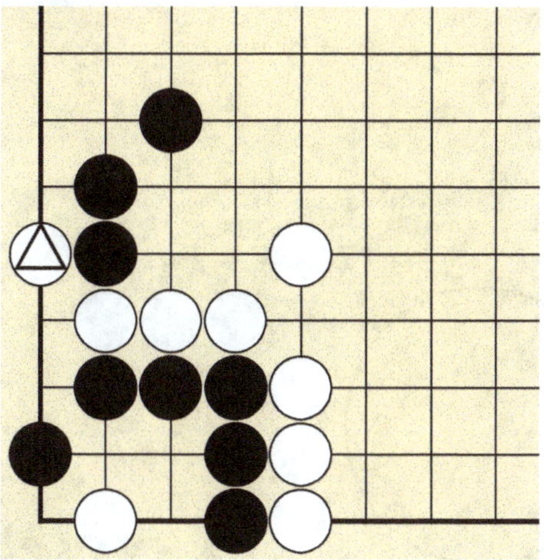

12

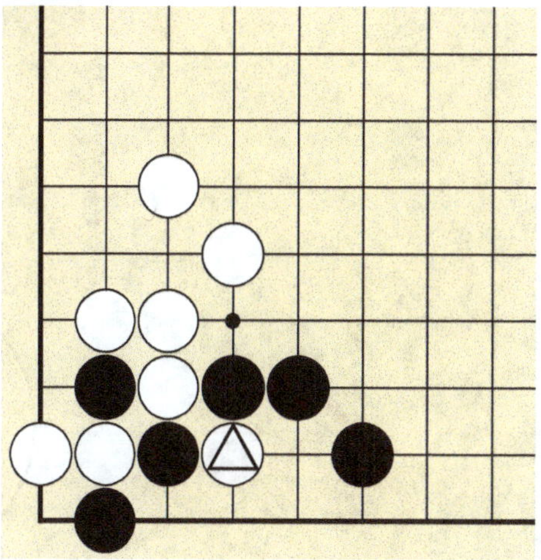

13

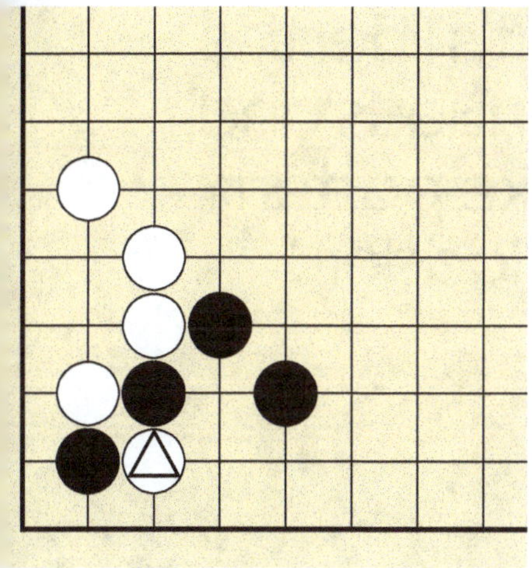

14

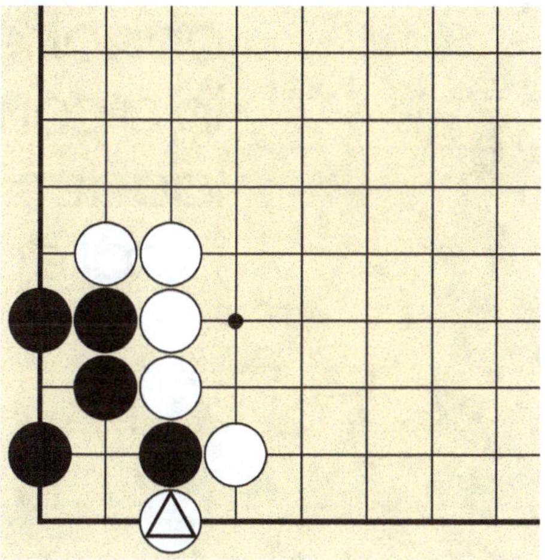

15

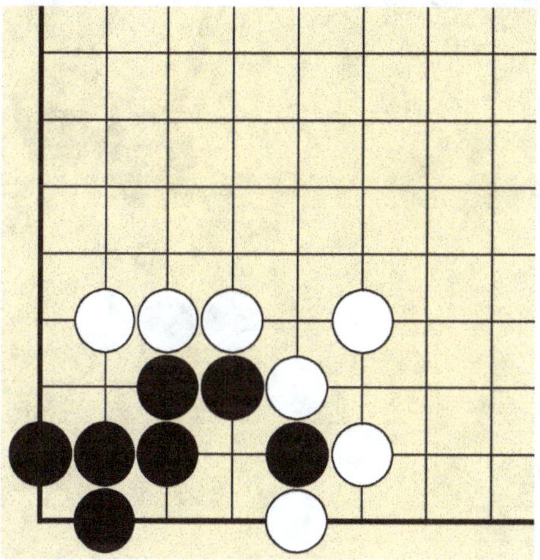

16

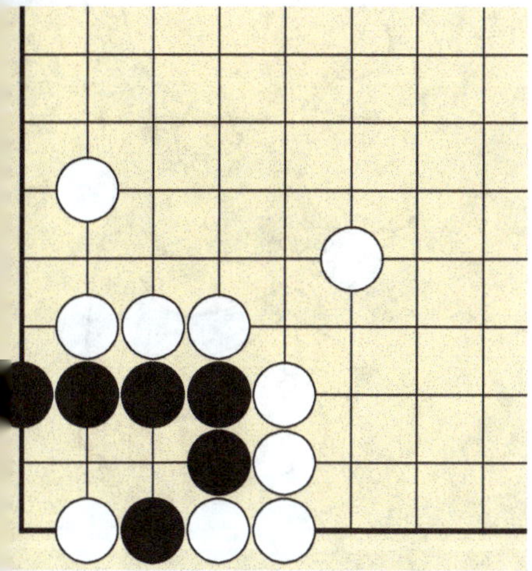

17

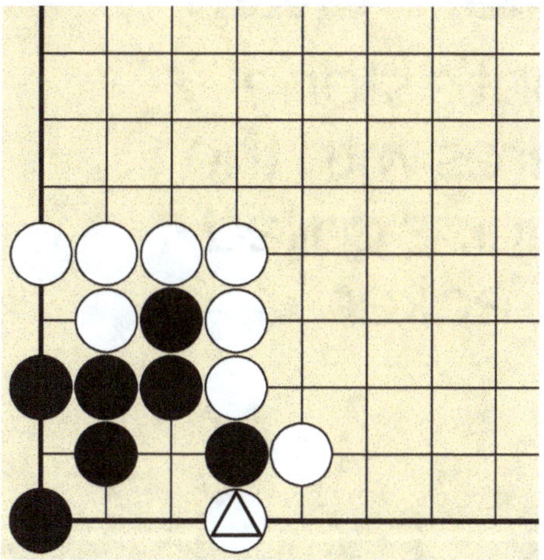

18

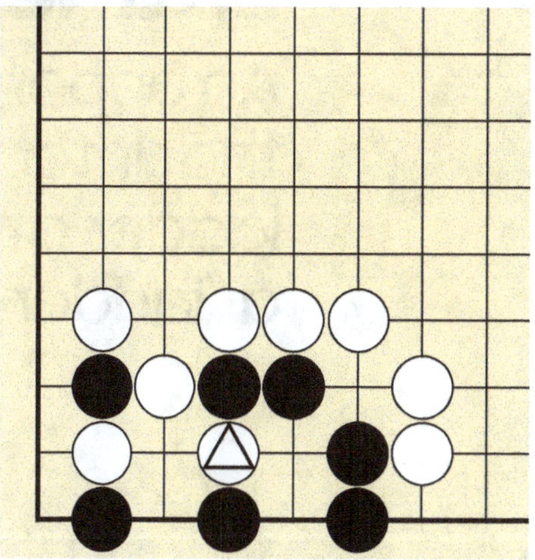

Fun Go Problems

Ladder

The technique of reducing the opponent's liberties in a continuous and ladder-like pattern is called "ladder."

Ladder Breaker

An opponent's stone that interferes with the ladder attack is called a "ladder breaker."

🦝 Ladder

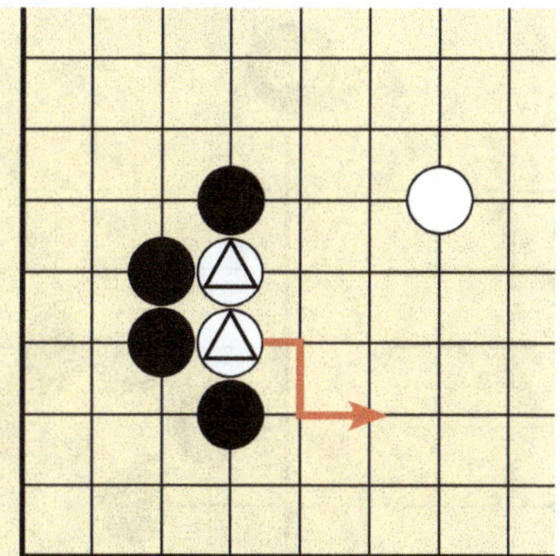

01 Draw a ladder-like pattern in the direction you want to drive the opponent.

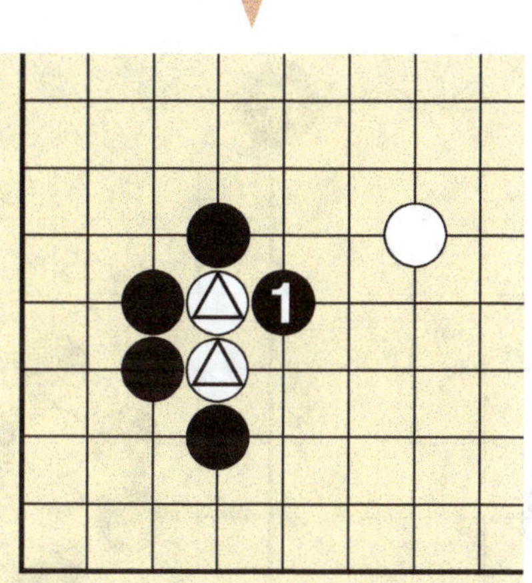

02 Driving the ladder toward an area without a ladder breaker is better.

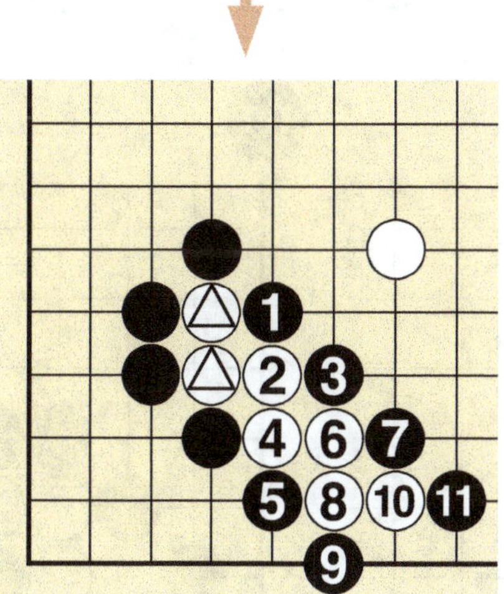

03 You can capture the opponent's stones by continuously blocking their liberties.

🦝 Ladder Breaker

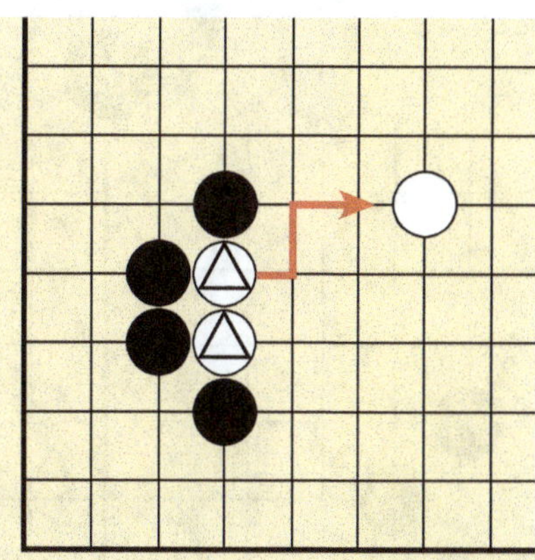

01 Draw a ladder-like pattern in the direction you want to drive the opponent.

02 Driving the ladder toward a ladder breaker is not a good strategy.

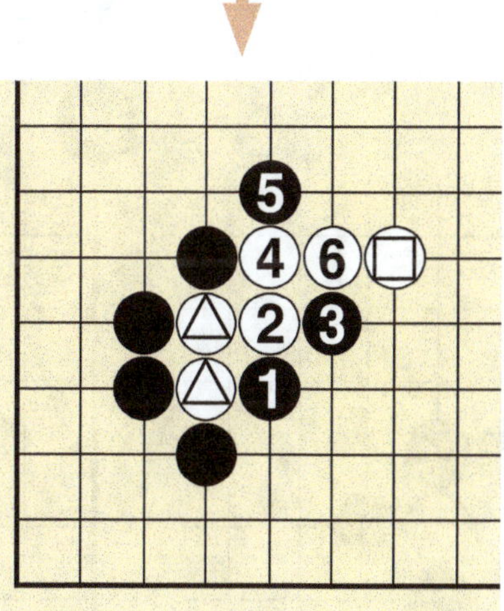

03 You cannot capture the opponent's stones even by continuously blocking their liberties.

Go For A Better World

? **Capture the white stones using the ladder technique.**

01

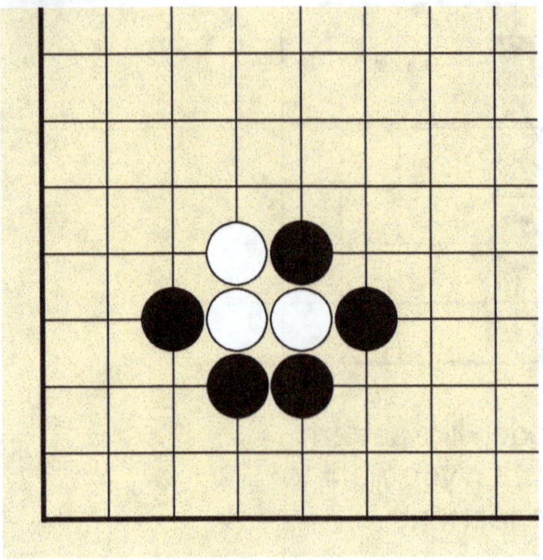

02

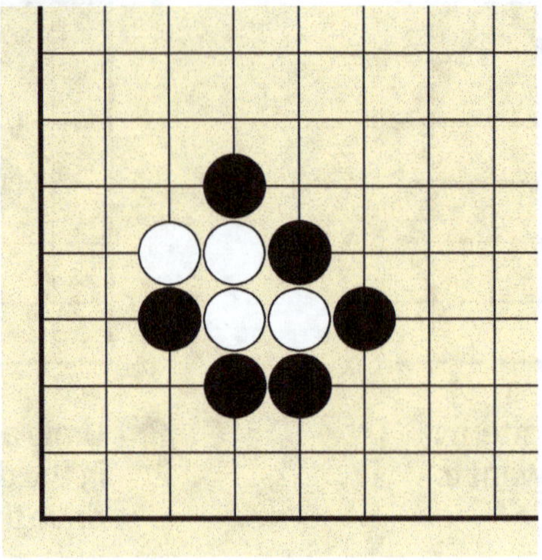

03

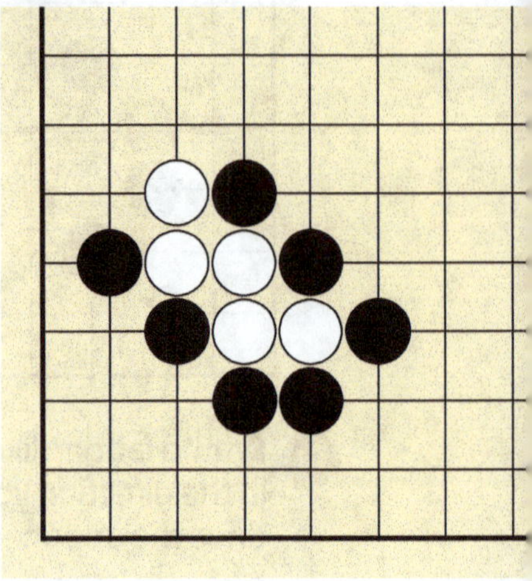

04

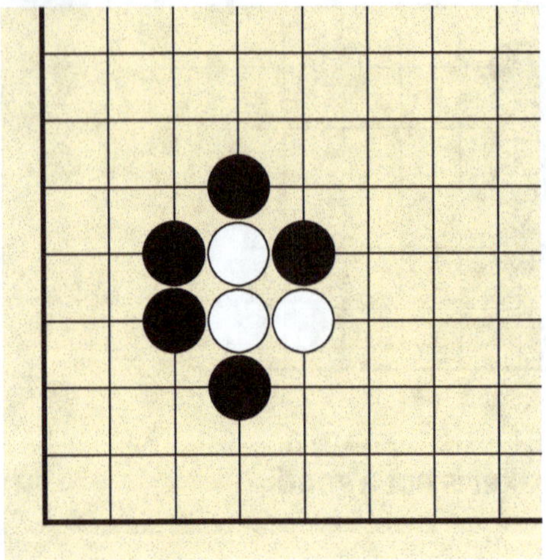

05

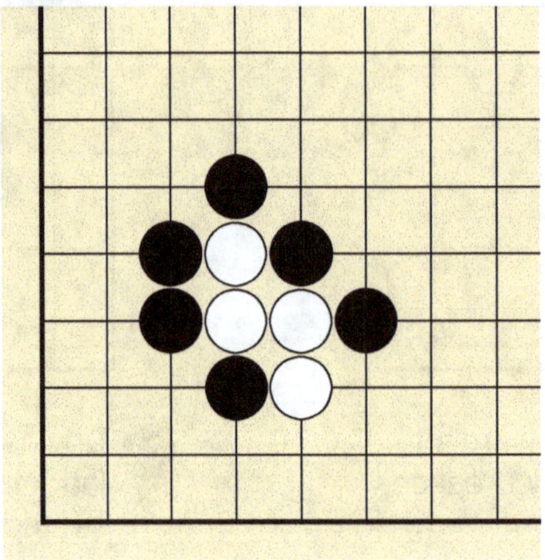

06

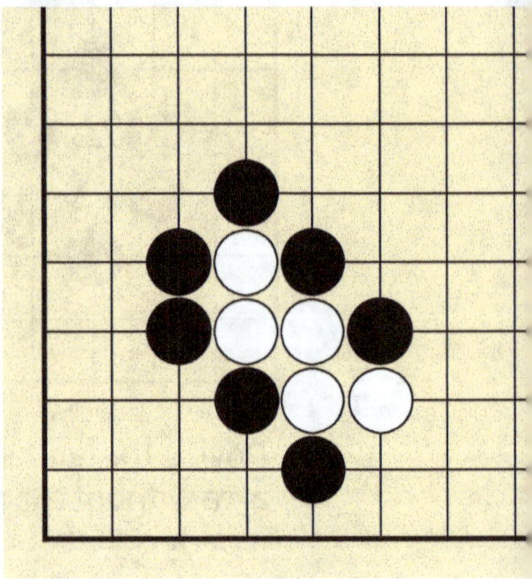

07

08

09

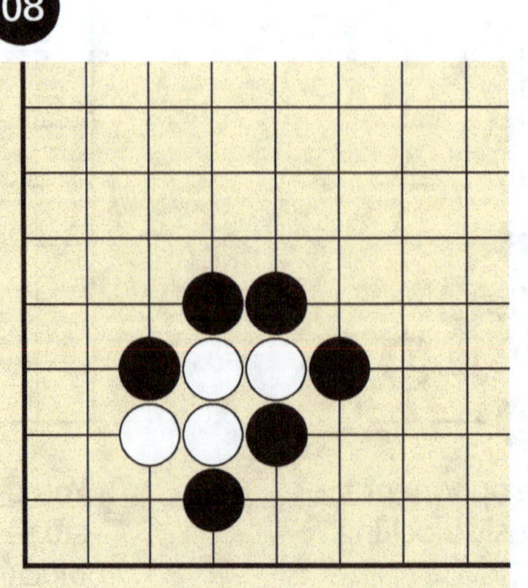

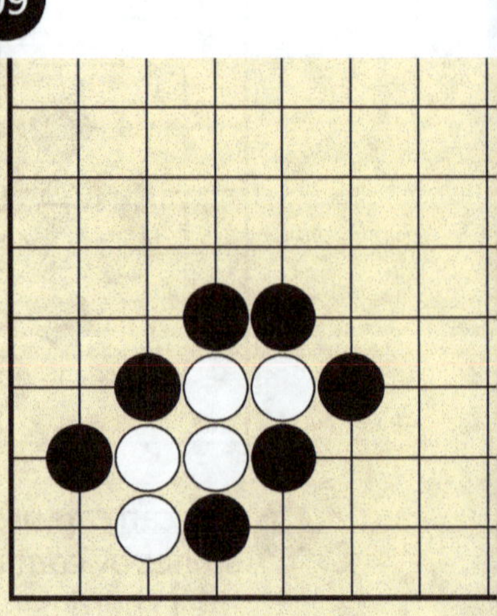

? Capture the white stones using the ladder technique.

10

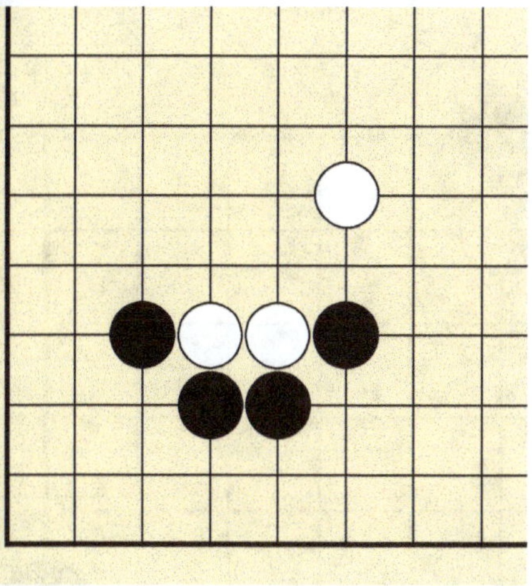

11

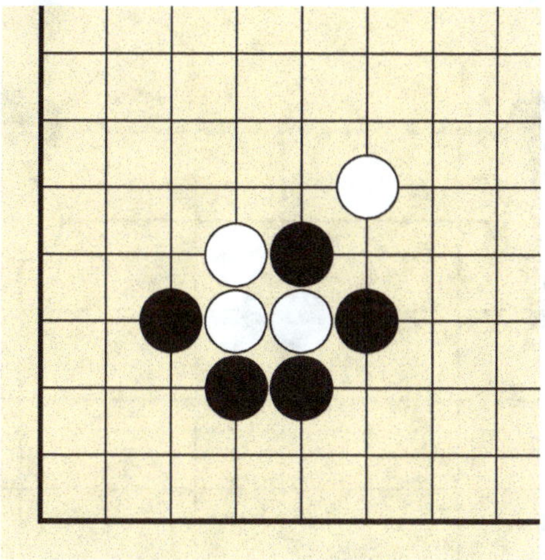

12

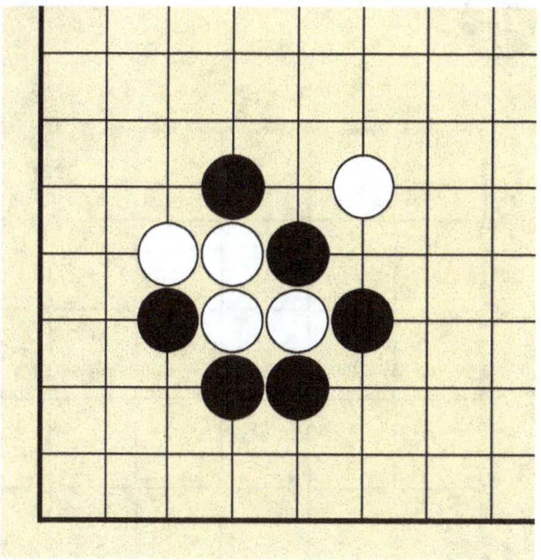

13

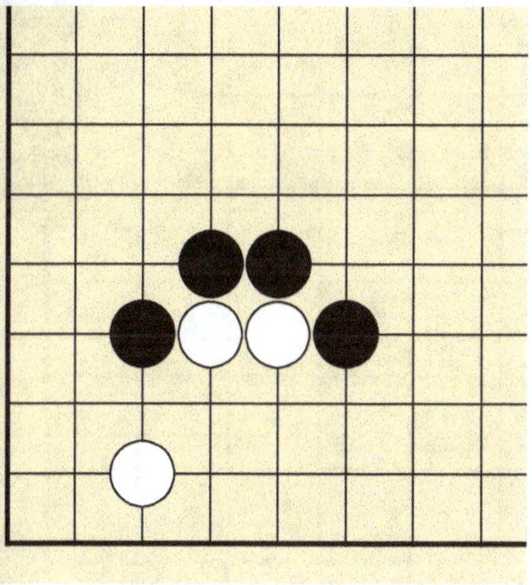

14

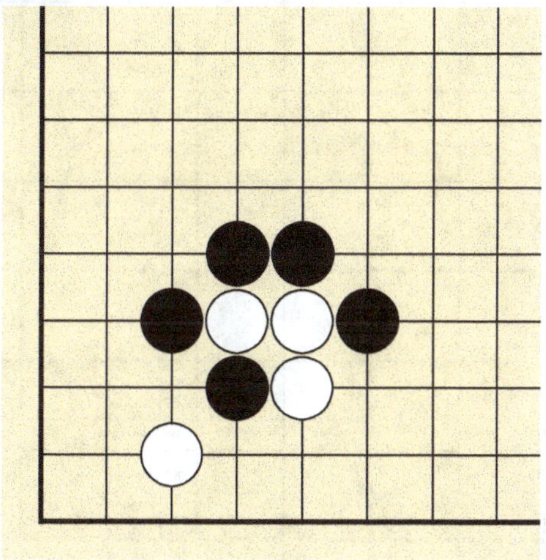

15

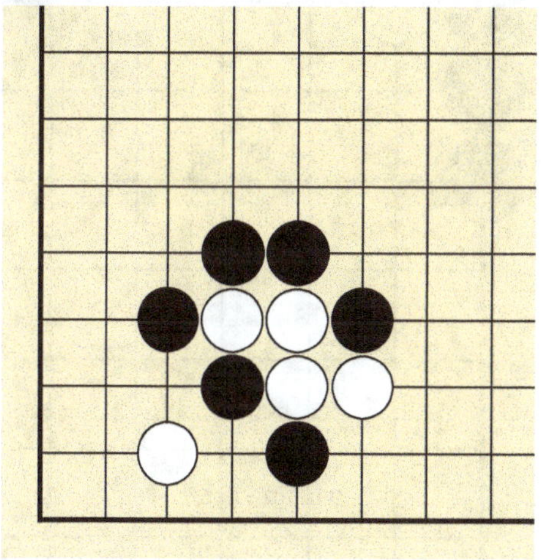

16

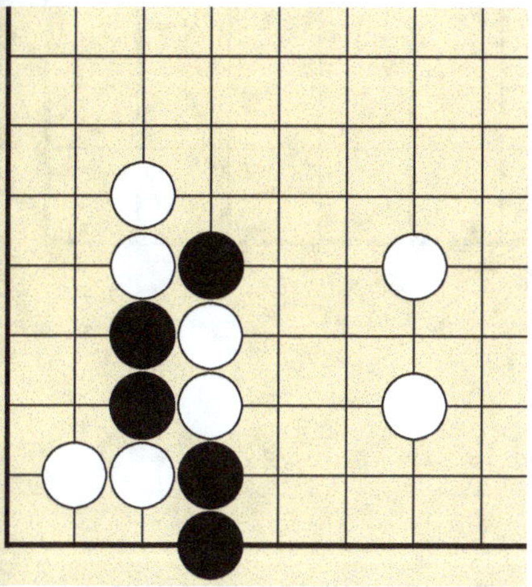

17

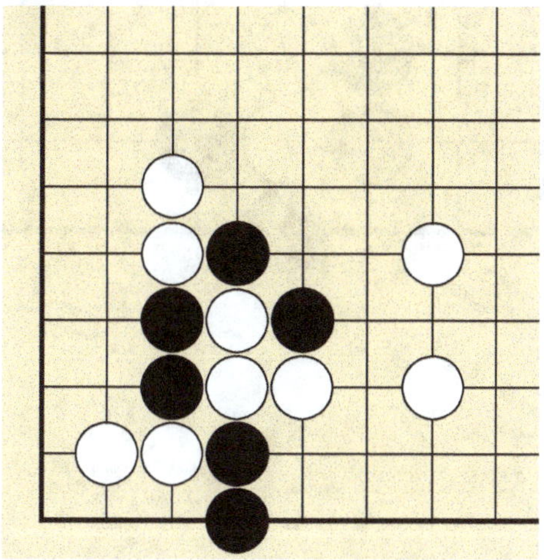

18

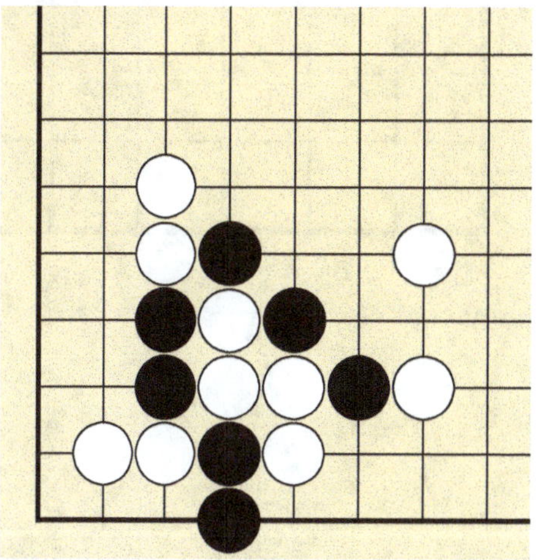

Black's Turn

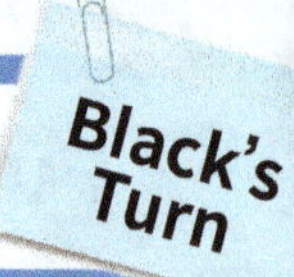

? Capture the white stones using the ladder technique.

When this pattern is completed, a heart shape will appear.

01

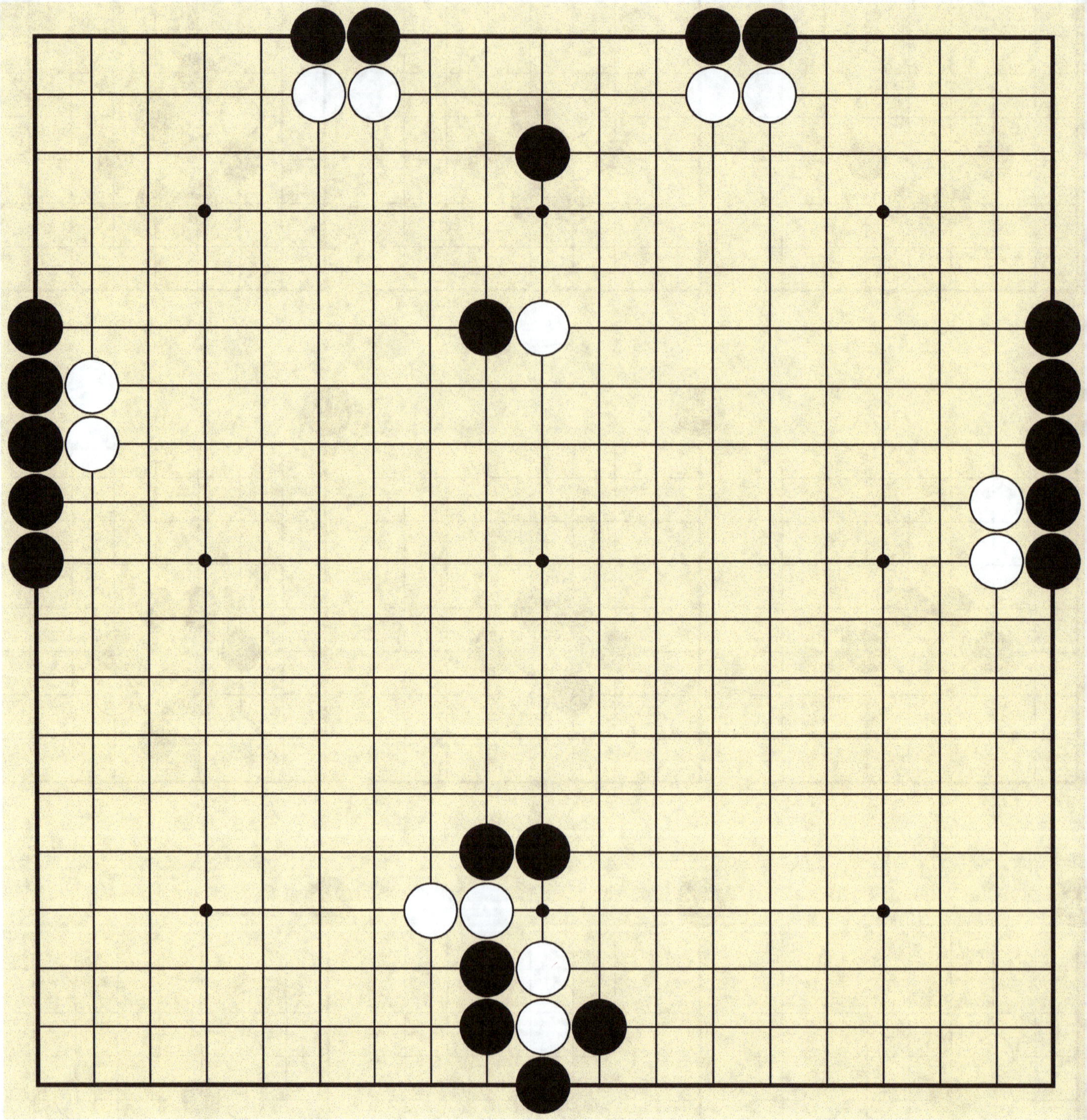

Closing Rules

Territories

Areas where black and white stones clearly surround each other are called "territories."

Neutral Points

An empty space that is not related to the outcome of the game is called a "neutral point."

⑤ Closing Rules _ ❶ Territories · ❷ Neutral Points

🐺 Territories

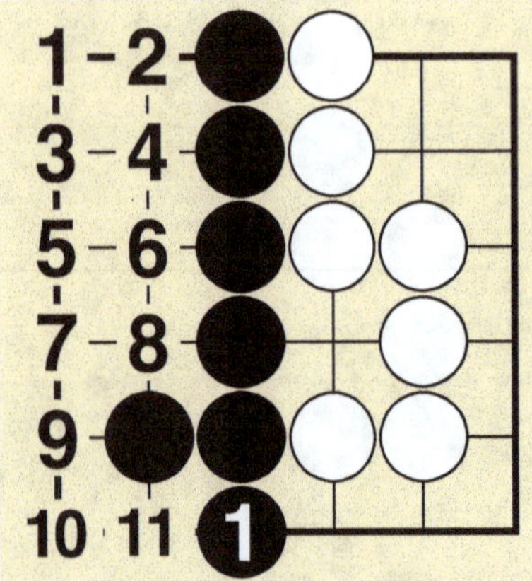

01 By placing a stone at Black 1, Black completed territories with 11 points.

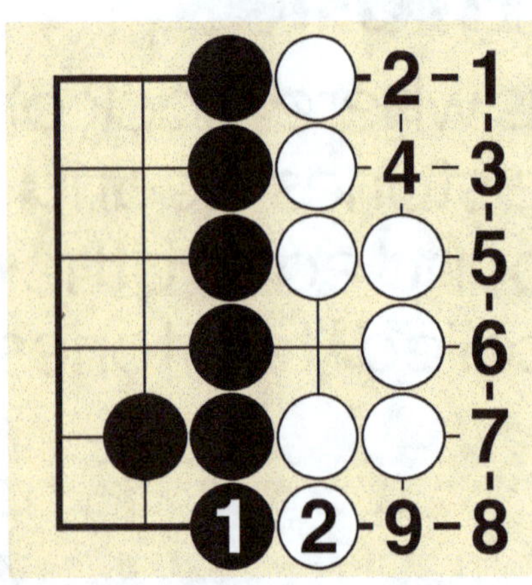

02 By placing a stone at White 2, White completed territories with 9 points.

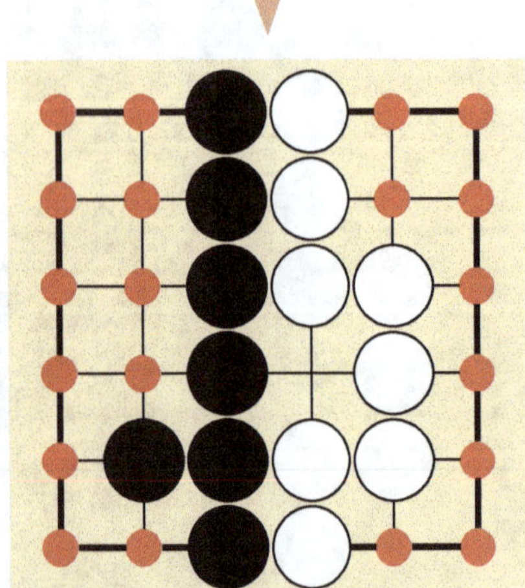

03 Black wins by 2 points (Black-11 points vs. White-9 points).

🐺 Neutral Points

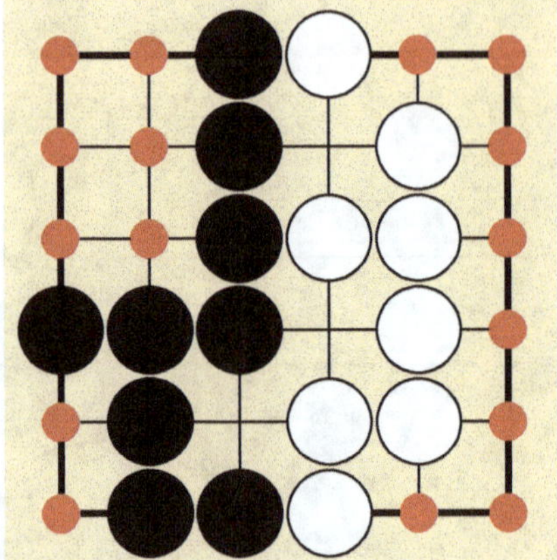

01 White and Black have 8 points each.

02 Black 1 and White 2 are neutral points, not related to the outcome of the game.

03 Black 3 is not a neutral point as it affects the outcome of the game.

Go For A Better World

5 Closing Rules _ 1 Territories

Black's Turn

? Place a black stone to fortify its territories.

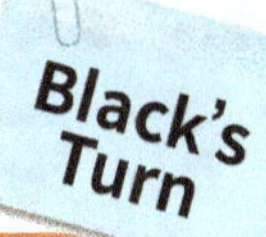

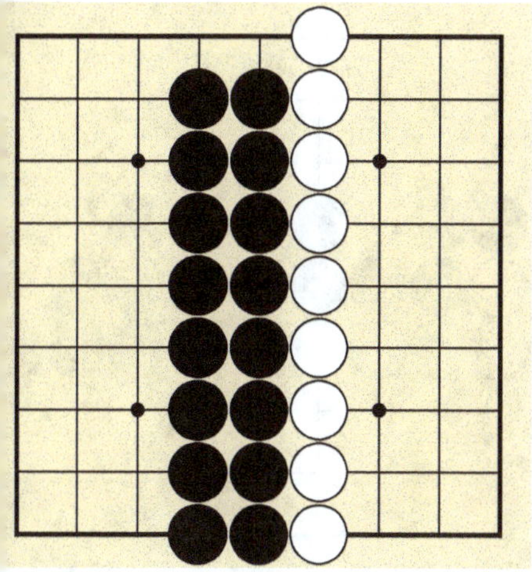

02

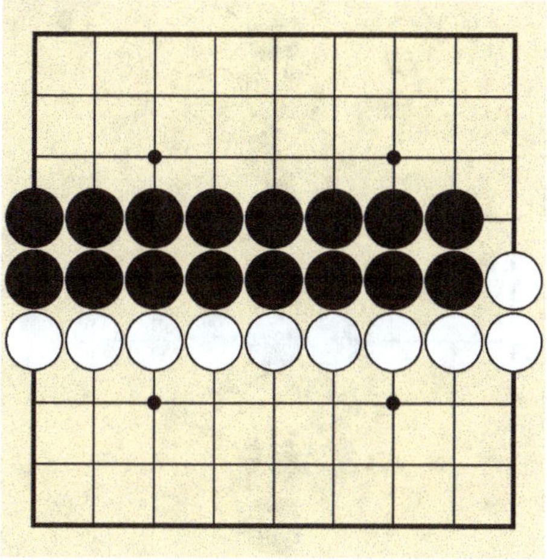

03

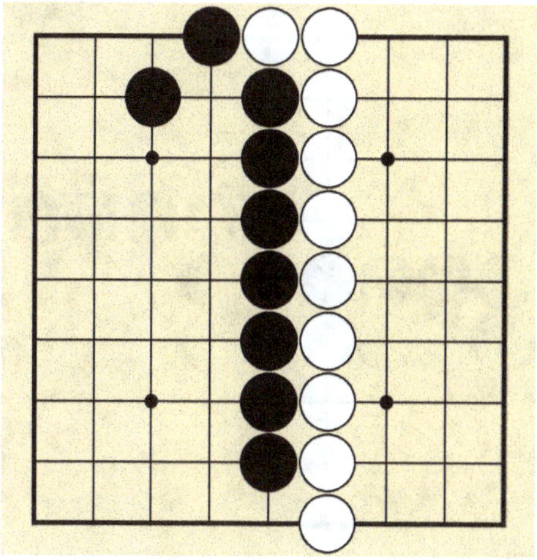

04

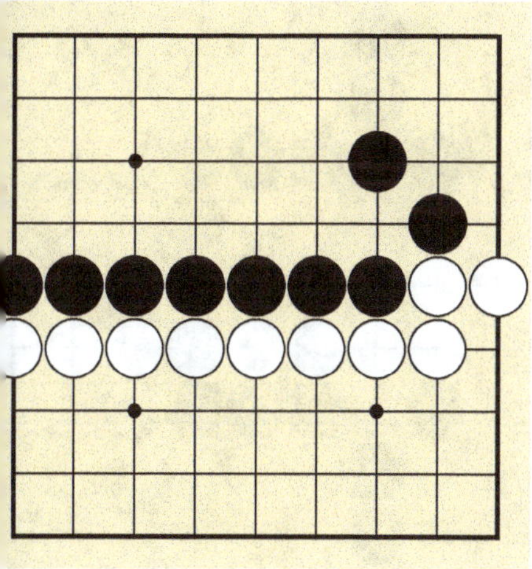

05

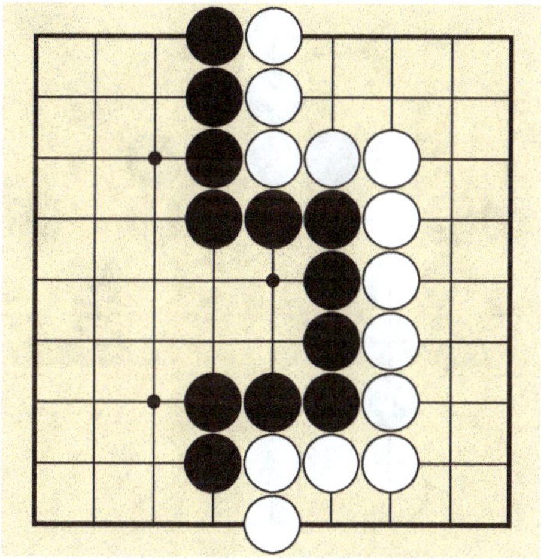

06

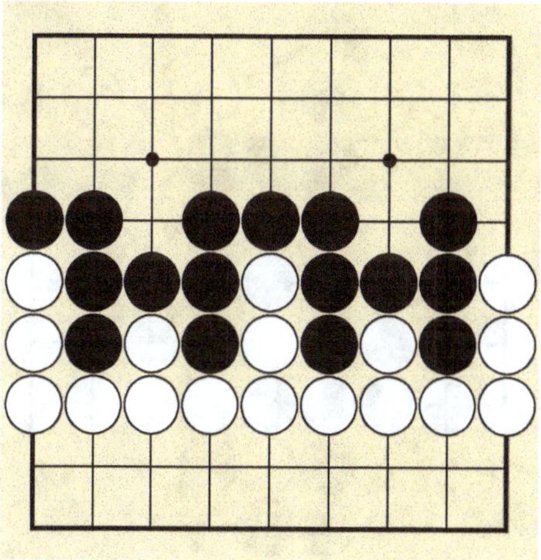

07

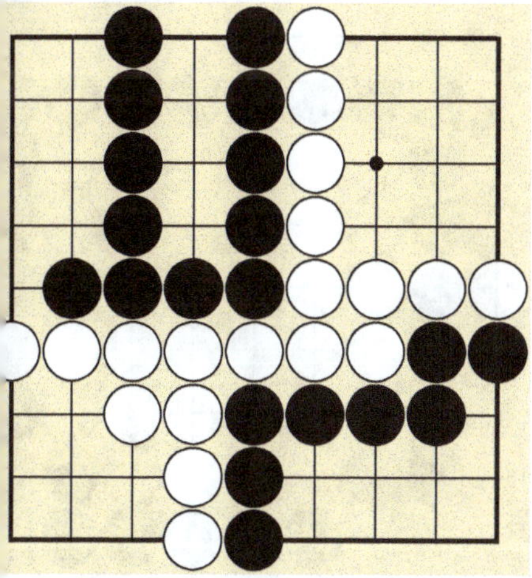

08

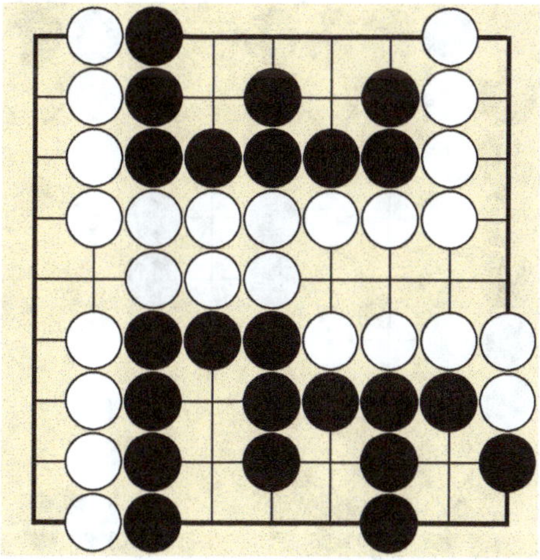

09

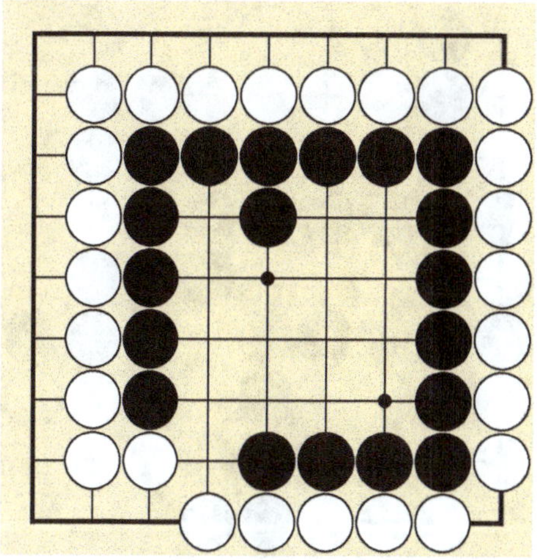

❺ Closing Rules _ ❶ Territories

Black's Turn

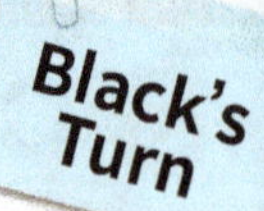

? Place a white stone to fortify its territories.

10

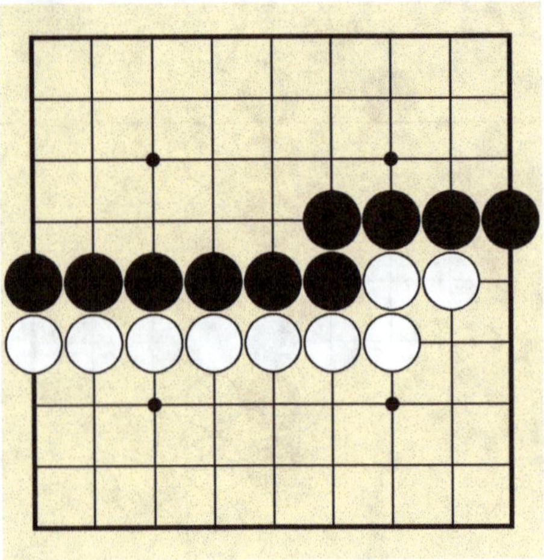

11

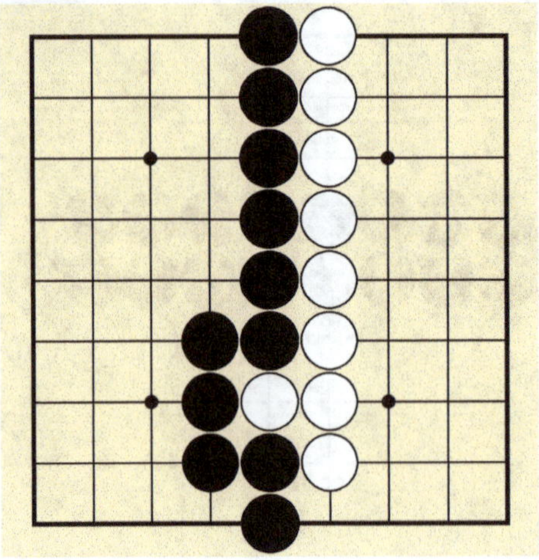

12

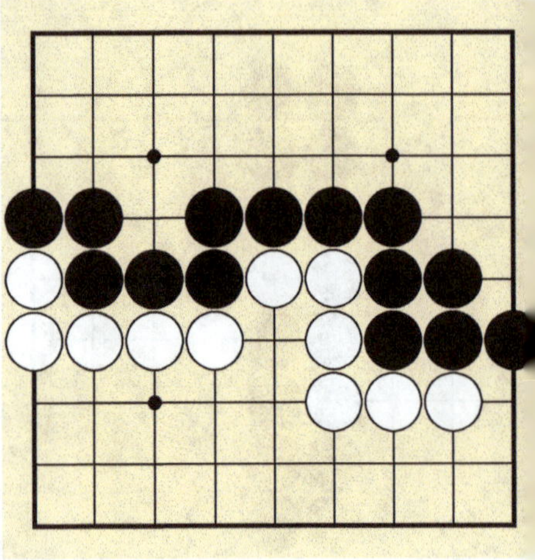

13

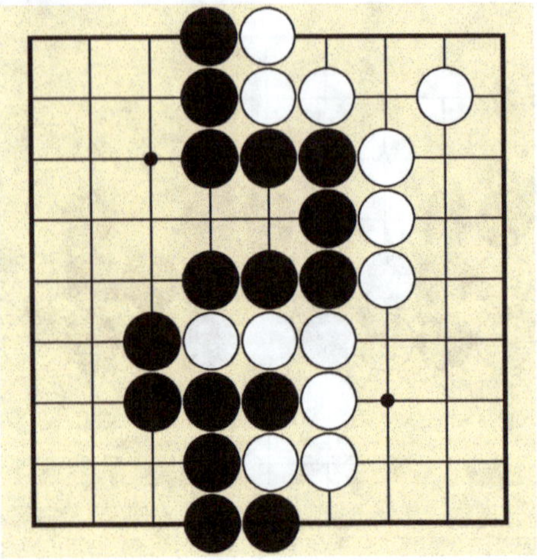

14

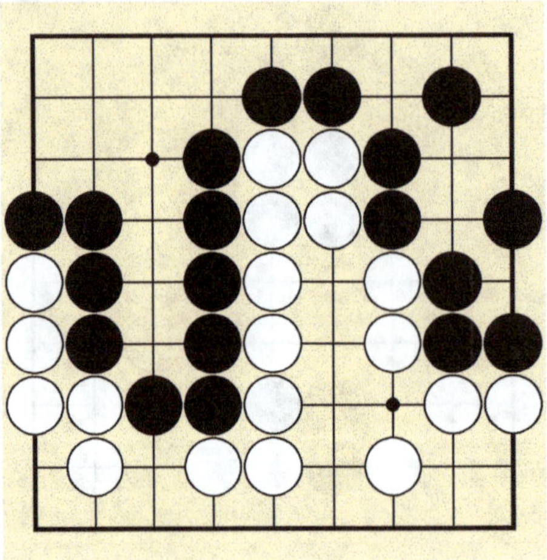

15

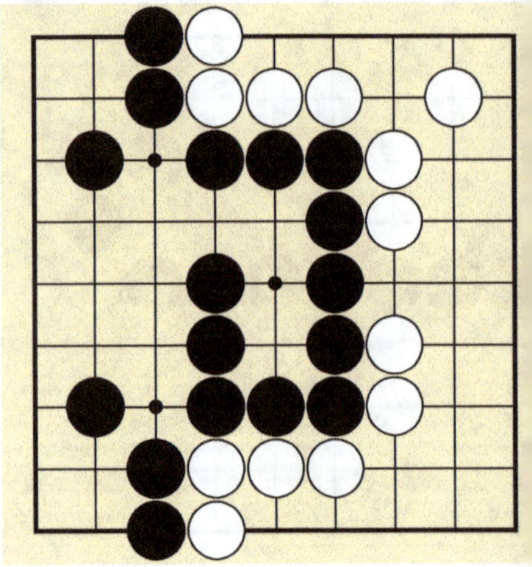

16

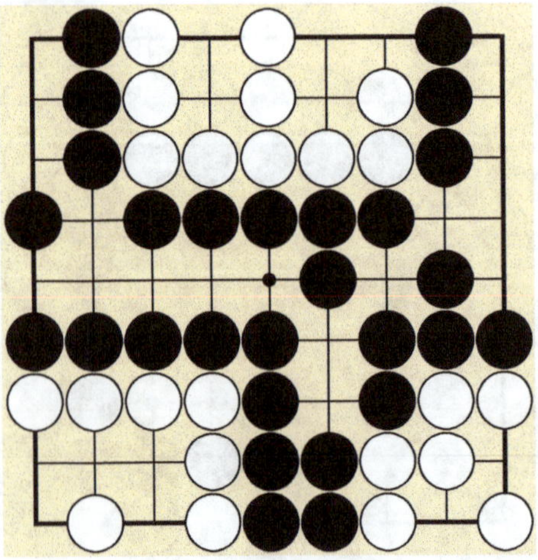

17

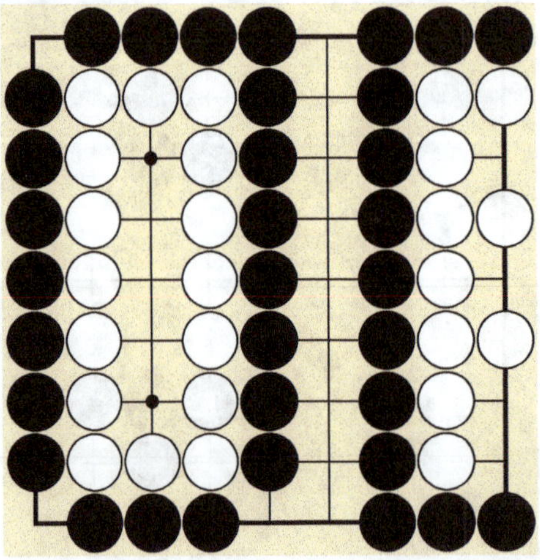

18

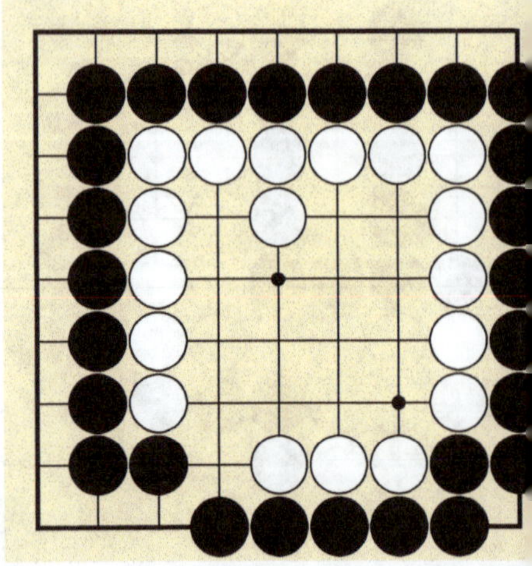

5 Closing Rules _ 2 Neutral Points

Black's Turn

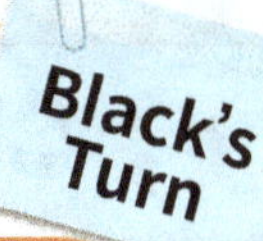

? Find the neutral points and mark them with "X"s.

01

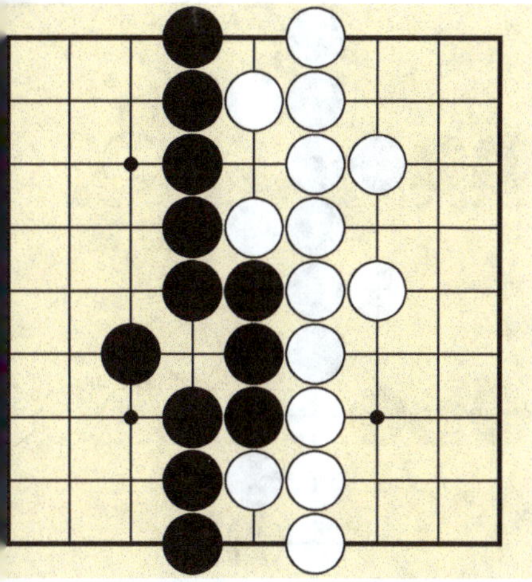

02

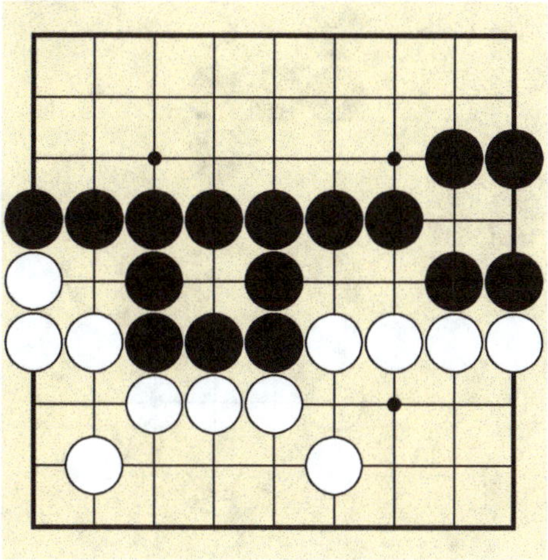

03

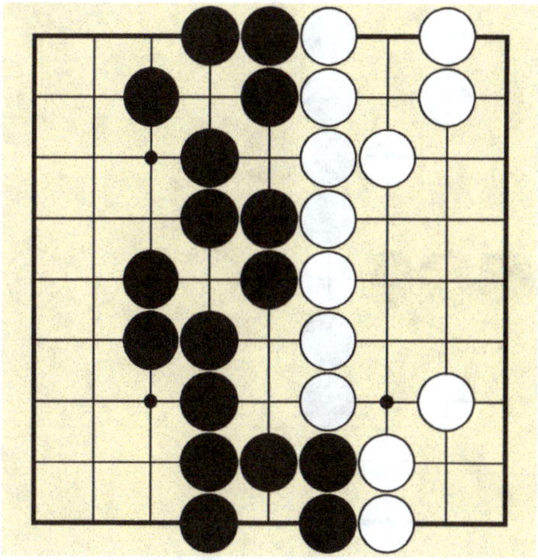

04

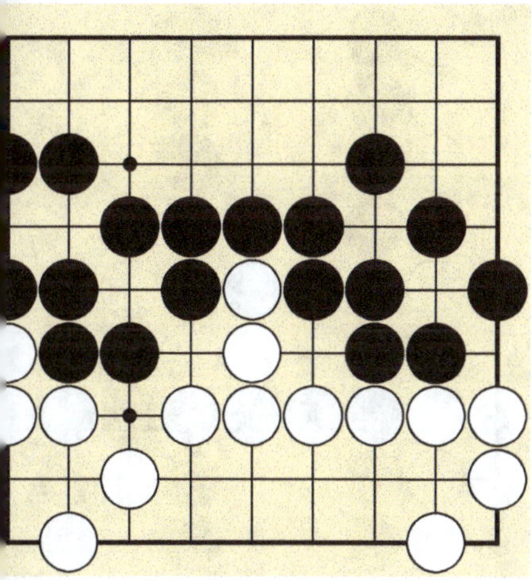

05

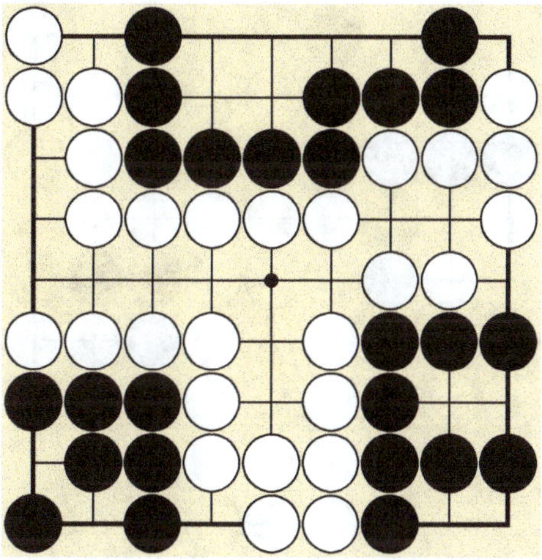

06

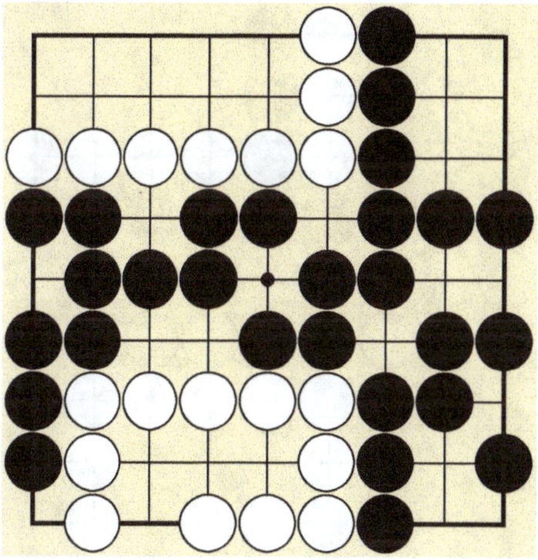

07

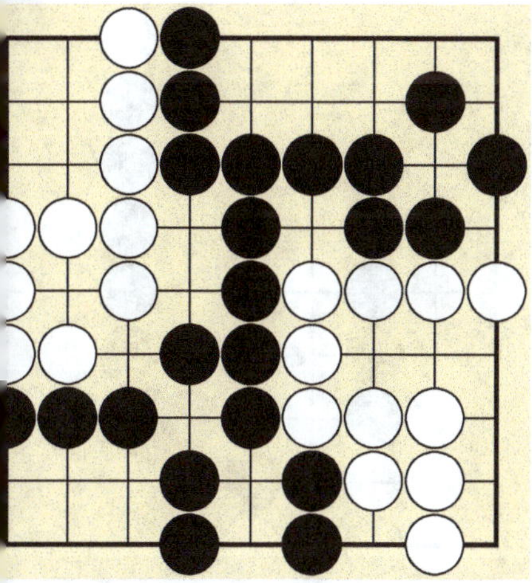

08

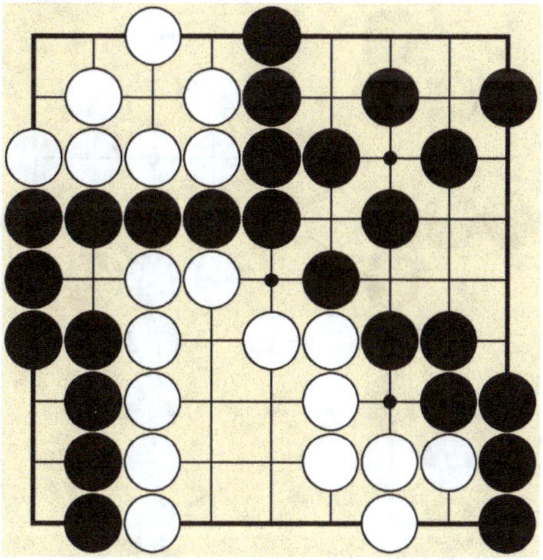

09

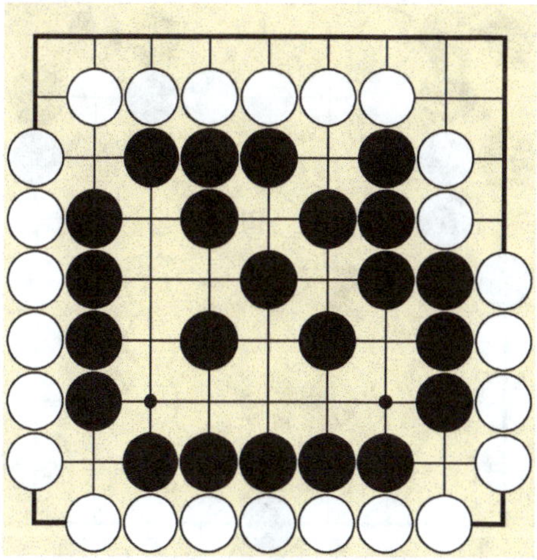

? Find the neutral points and mark them with "X"s.

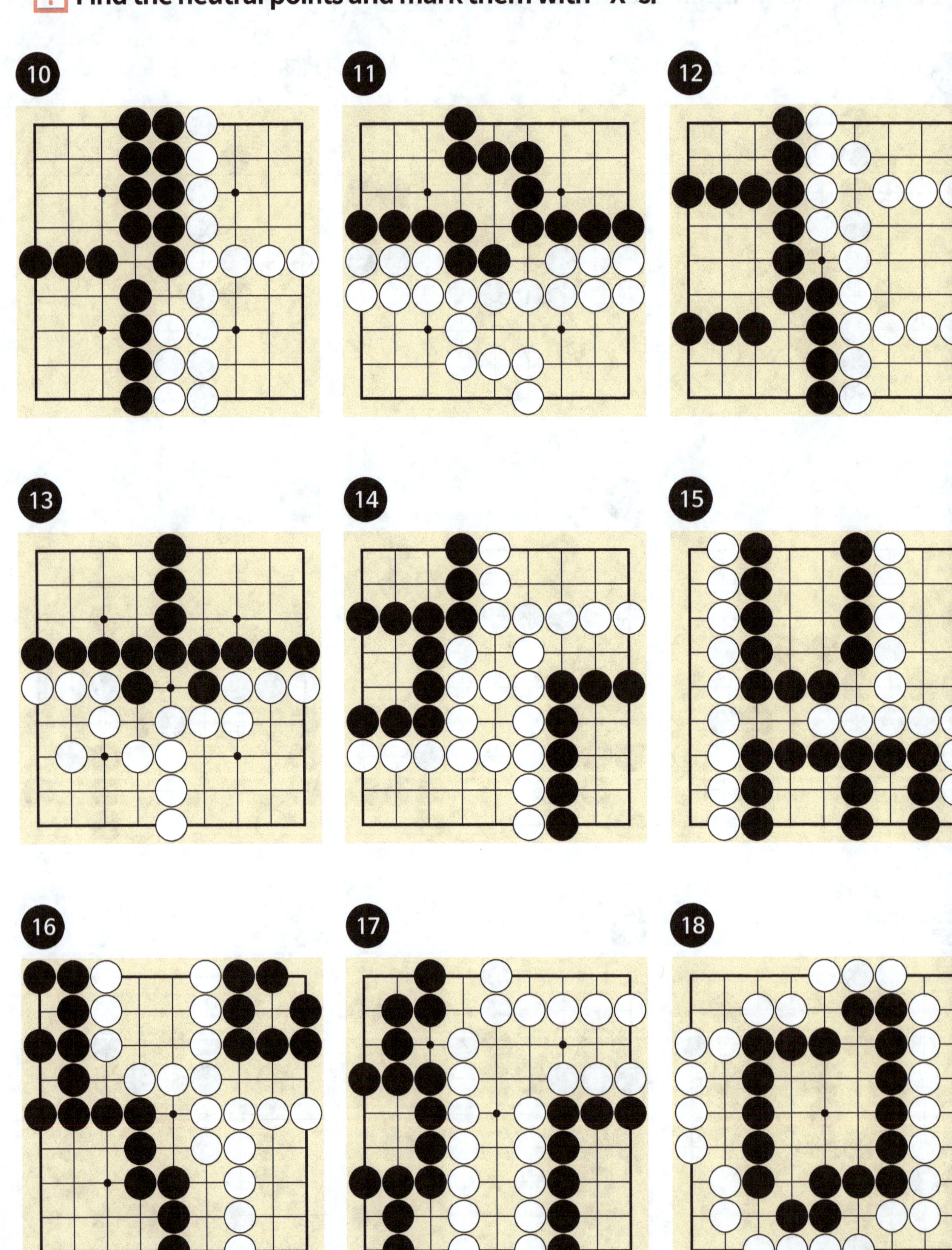

Appendix. Understanding the Go board

? Write down the correct names of the areas on a Go board.

01

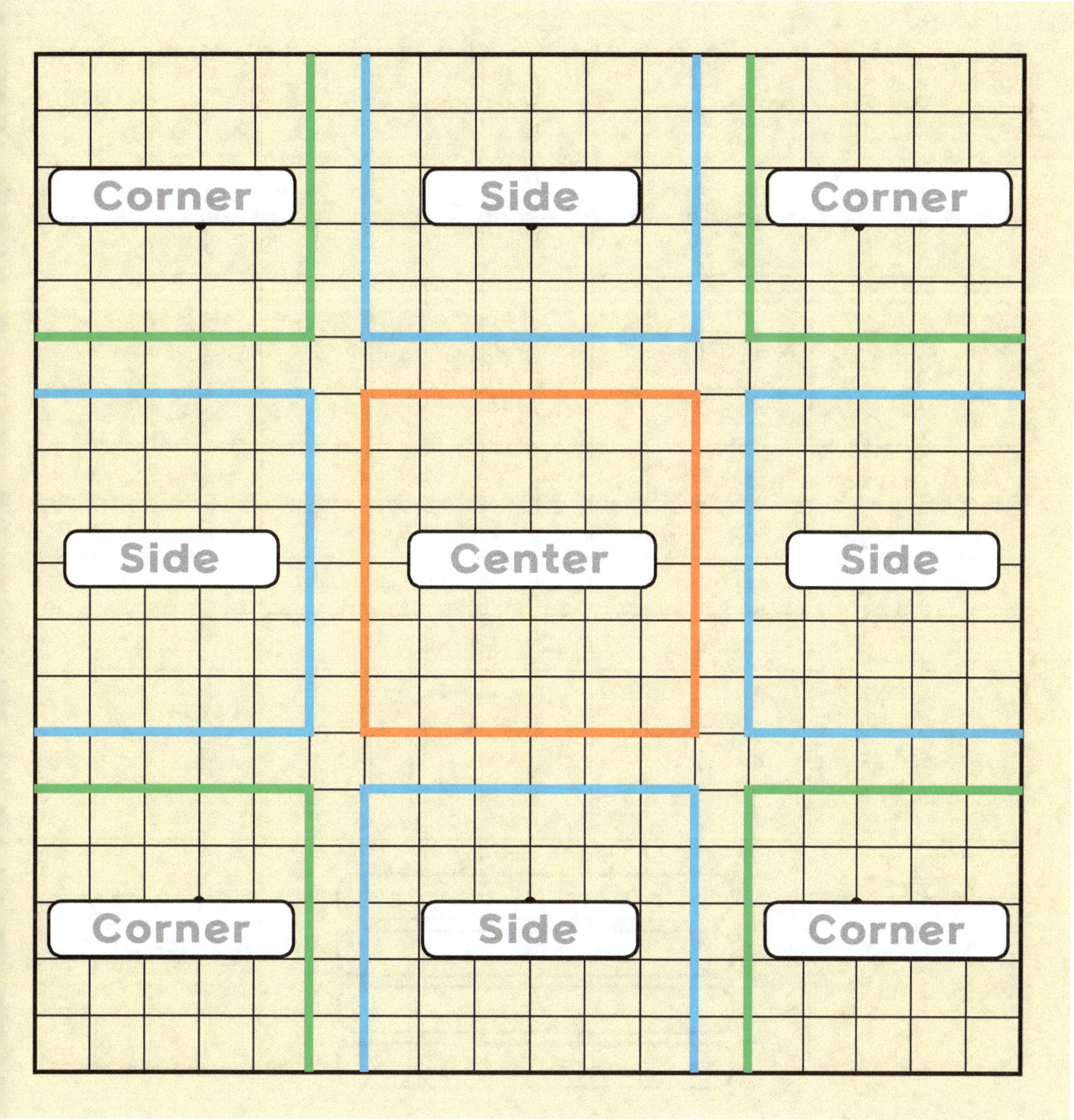

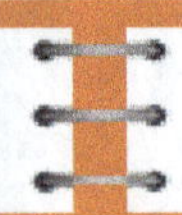

Appendix. Understanding the Go board

? Write down the correct names of the lines on a Go board.

02

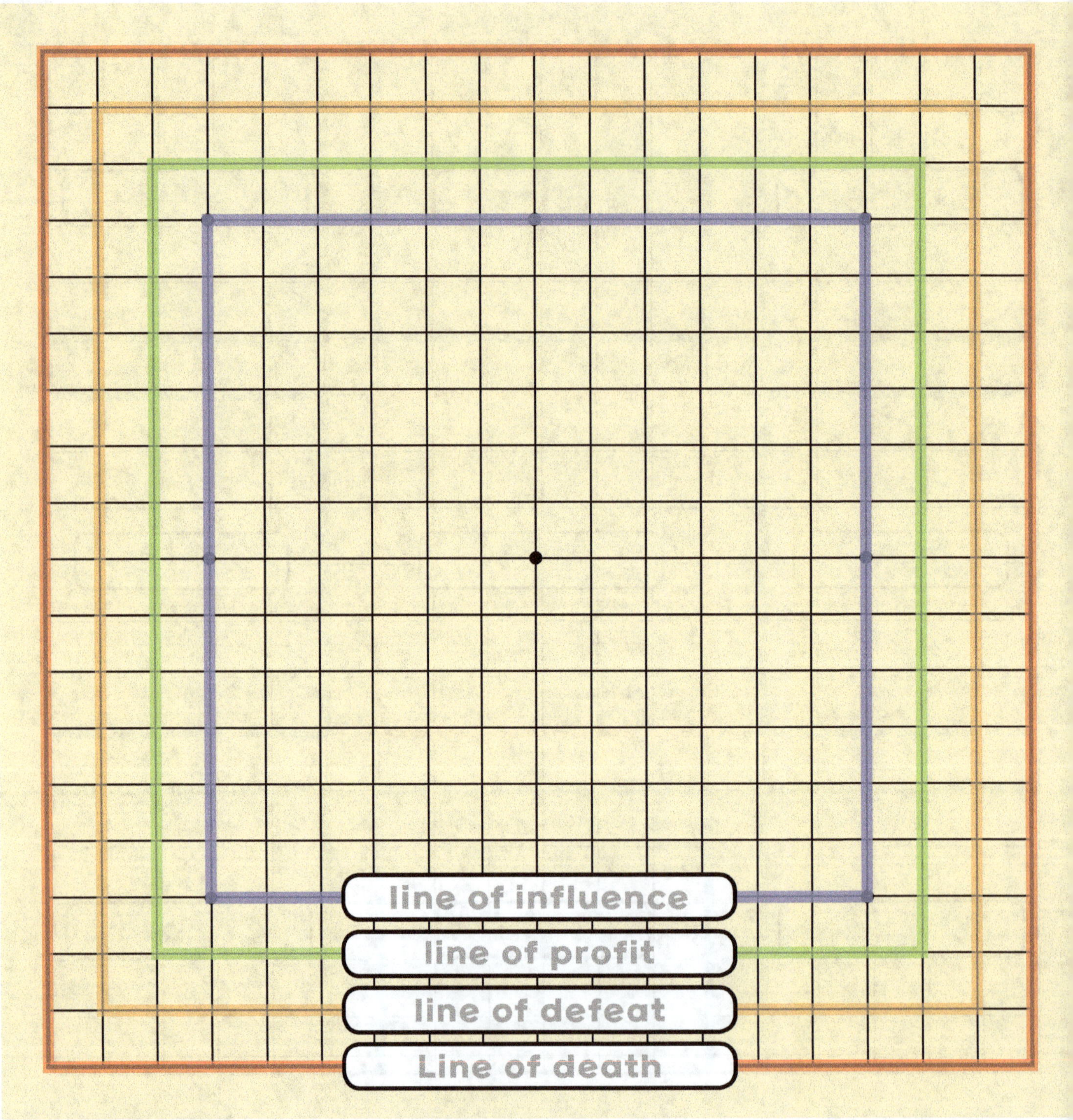

APPLY FOR "GTGO MENTOR" CERTIFICATION

Congratulations!
You have successfully completed the introductory Go course through the Gateway to Go curriculum. Now, take the next step by applying for the "GTGO Mentor" certification and become a leader within the Gateway to Go community.

How to Apply for the 'GTGO Mentor' Certification

1

2

3

Scan the QR Code

Scan the QR code included in the curriculum to access the 'GTGO Mentor' application site.

Submit Application

Once on the site, enter some basic information to apply for your certification.

Receive Certification via Email

After submitting your application, the certification will be sent to you via email.

Benefits for 'GTGO Mentor' Certificate Holders

1

2

Gateway to Go Instructor Activities

Those who hold the 'GTGO Mentor' certification can lead the introductory education courses of Gateway to Go.

Gateway to Go Global Membership

Become a member of the Gateway to Go global community and interact with other 'GTGO Mentors.'
You can also participate as a leader in activities aimed at expanding the Go community.

GTGO Mentor Certificate Example

gatewaytogo.org

01

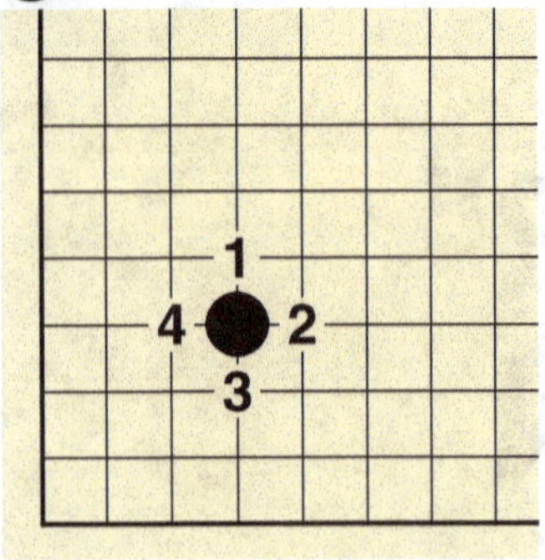

02

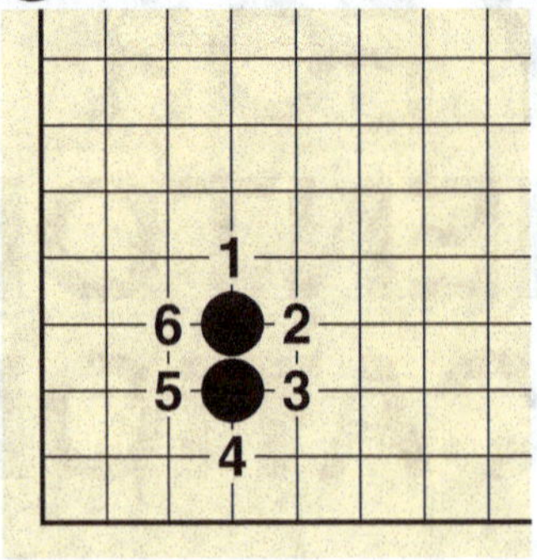

03

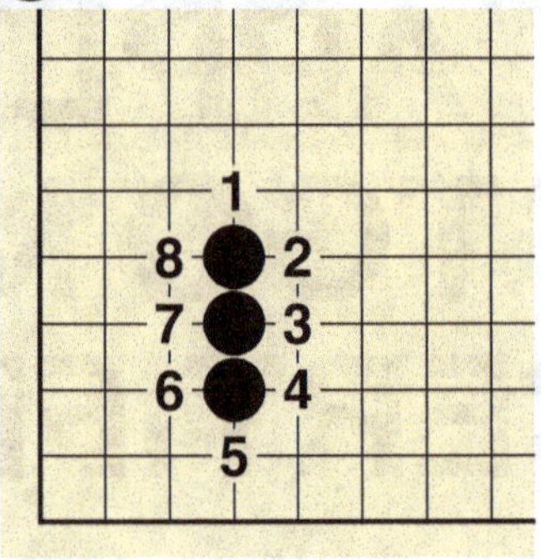

04

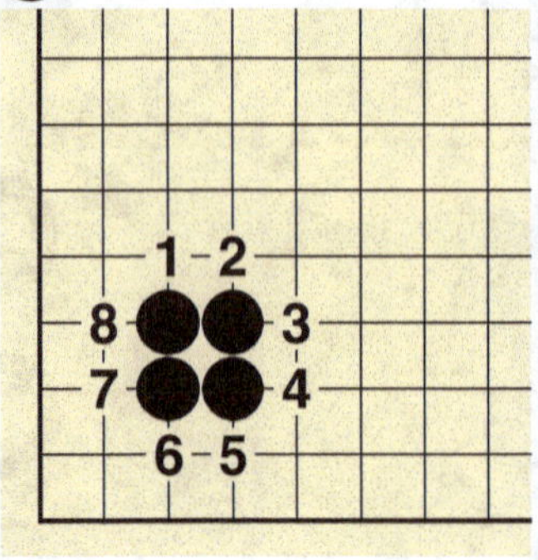

05

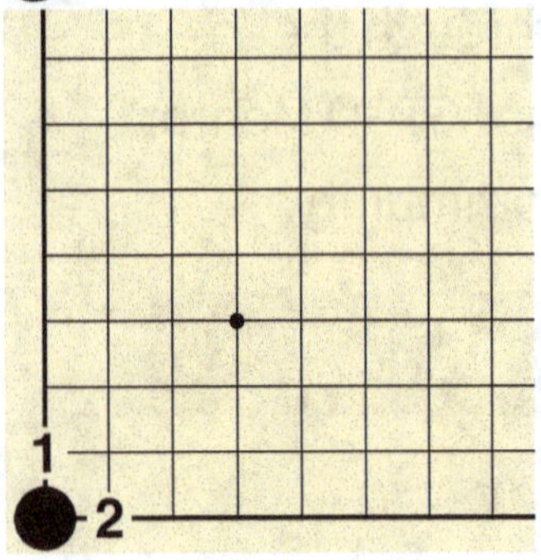

06

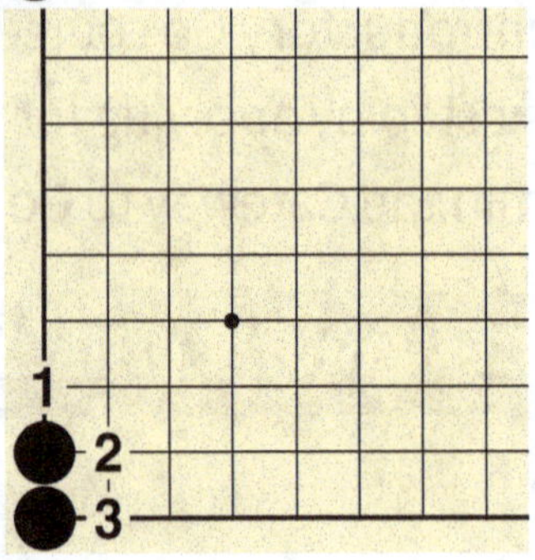

07

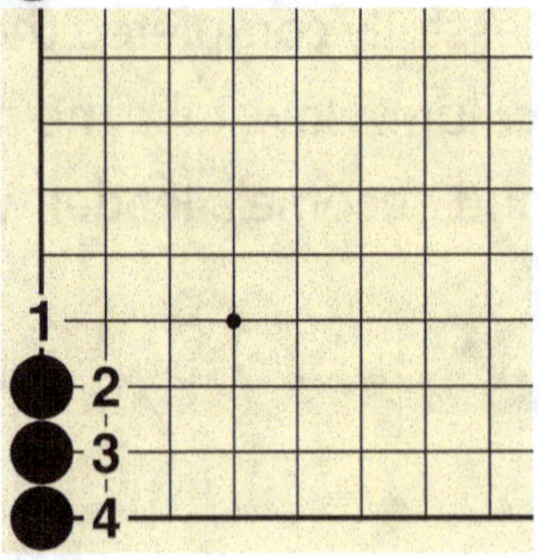

08

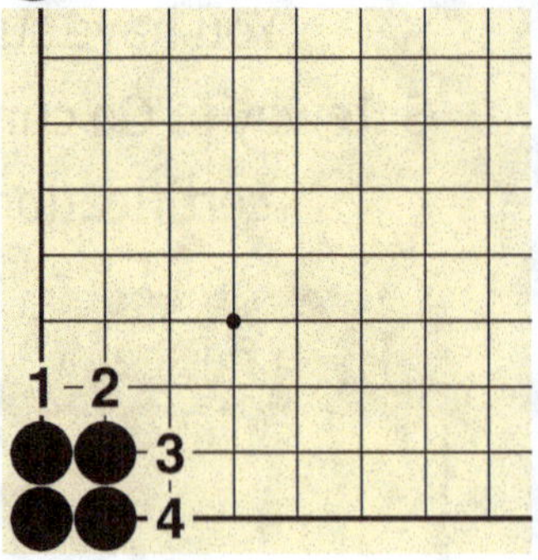

09

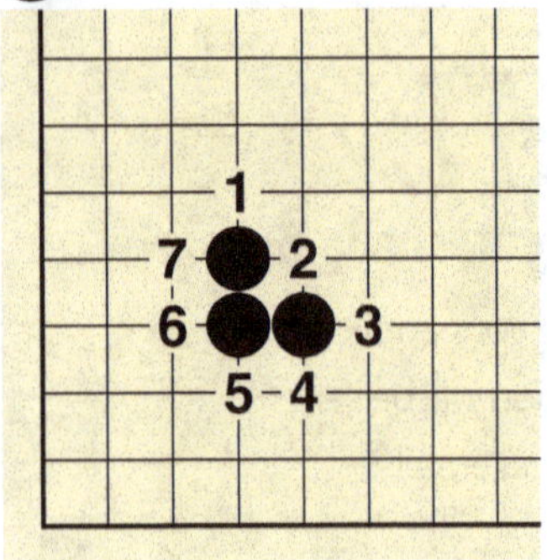

10

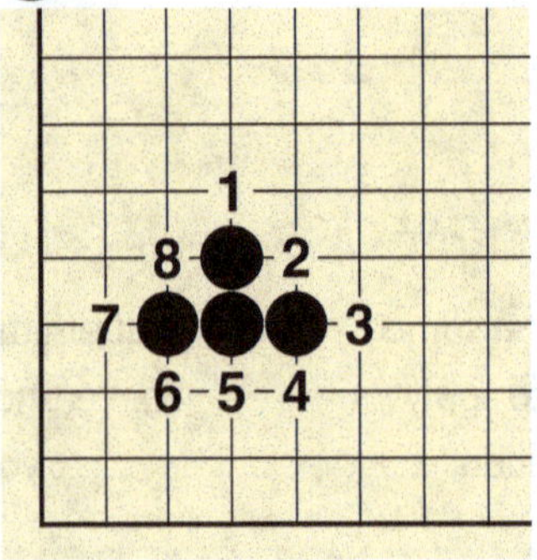

11

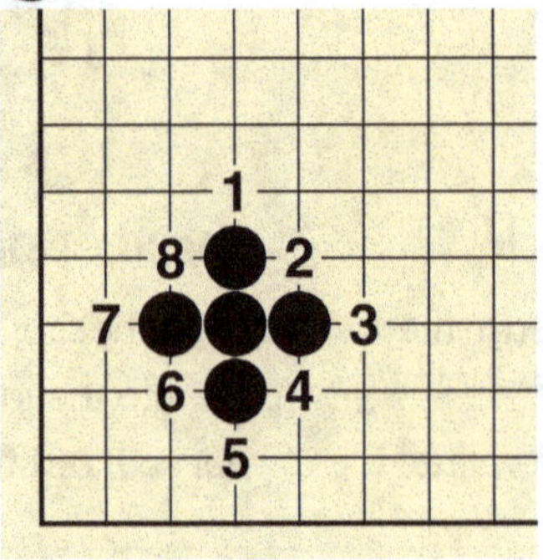

12

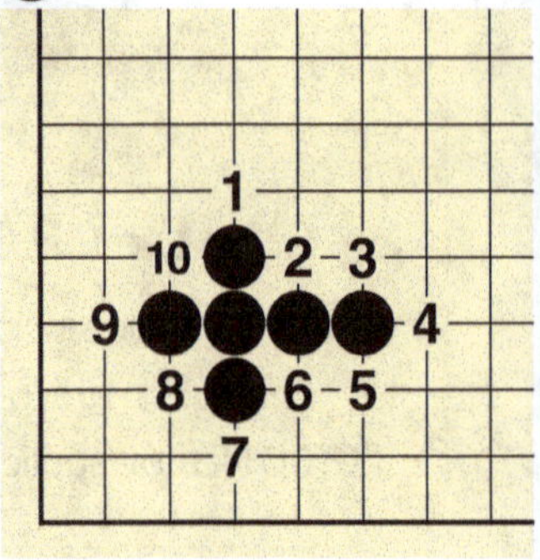

13

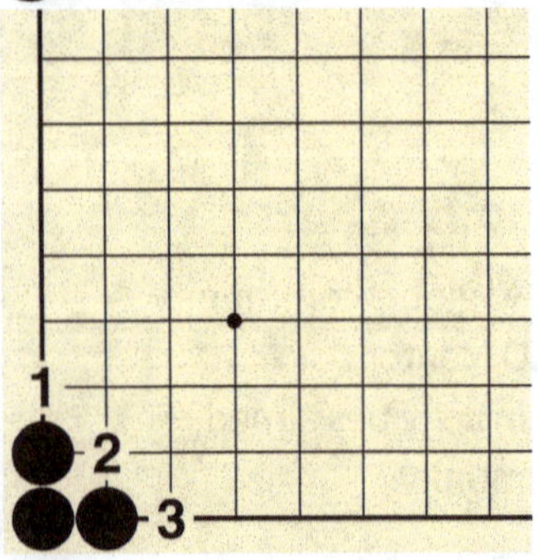

14

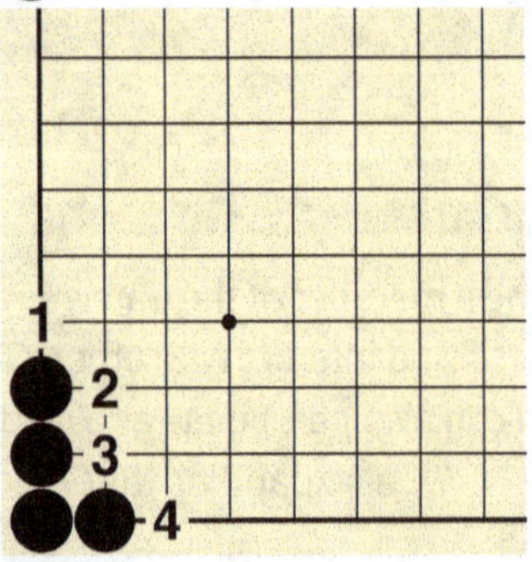

15

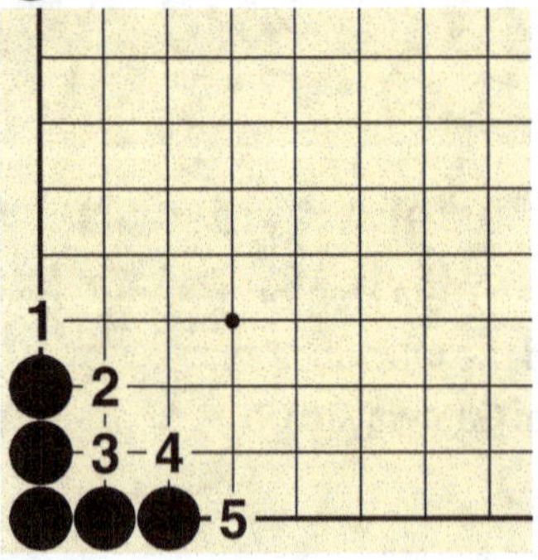

16

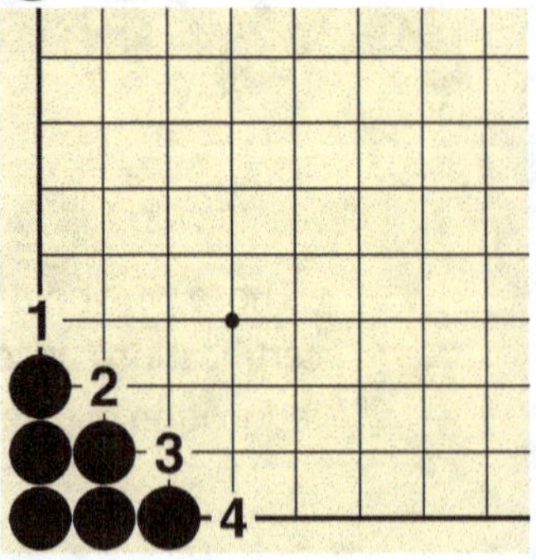

17

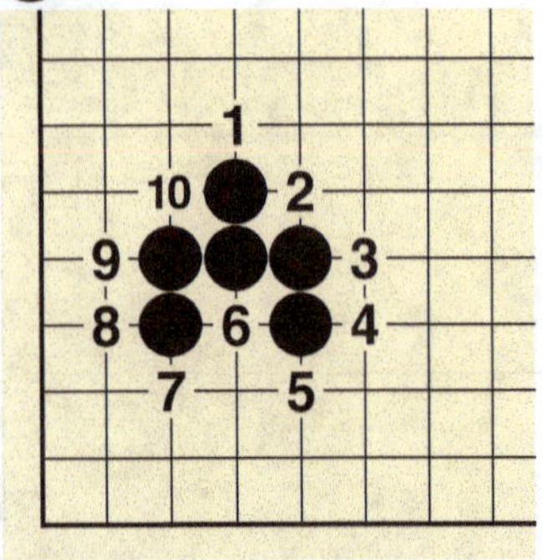

18

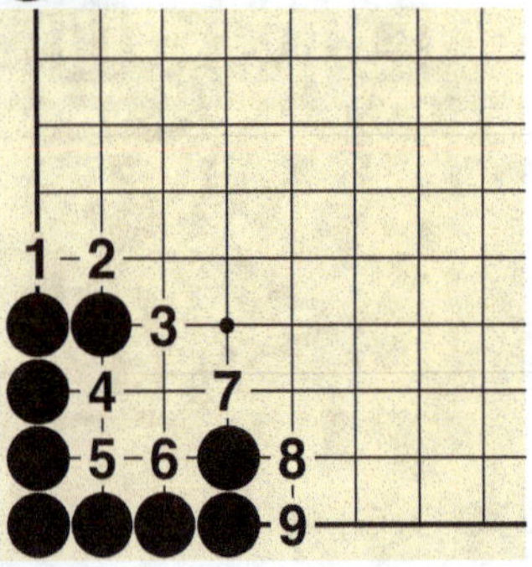

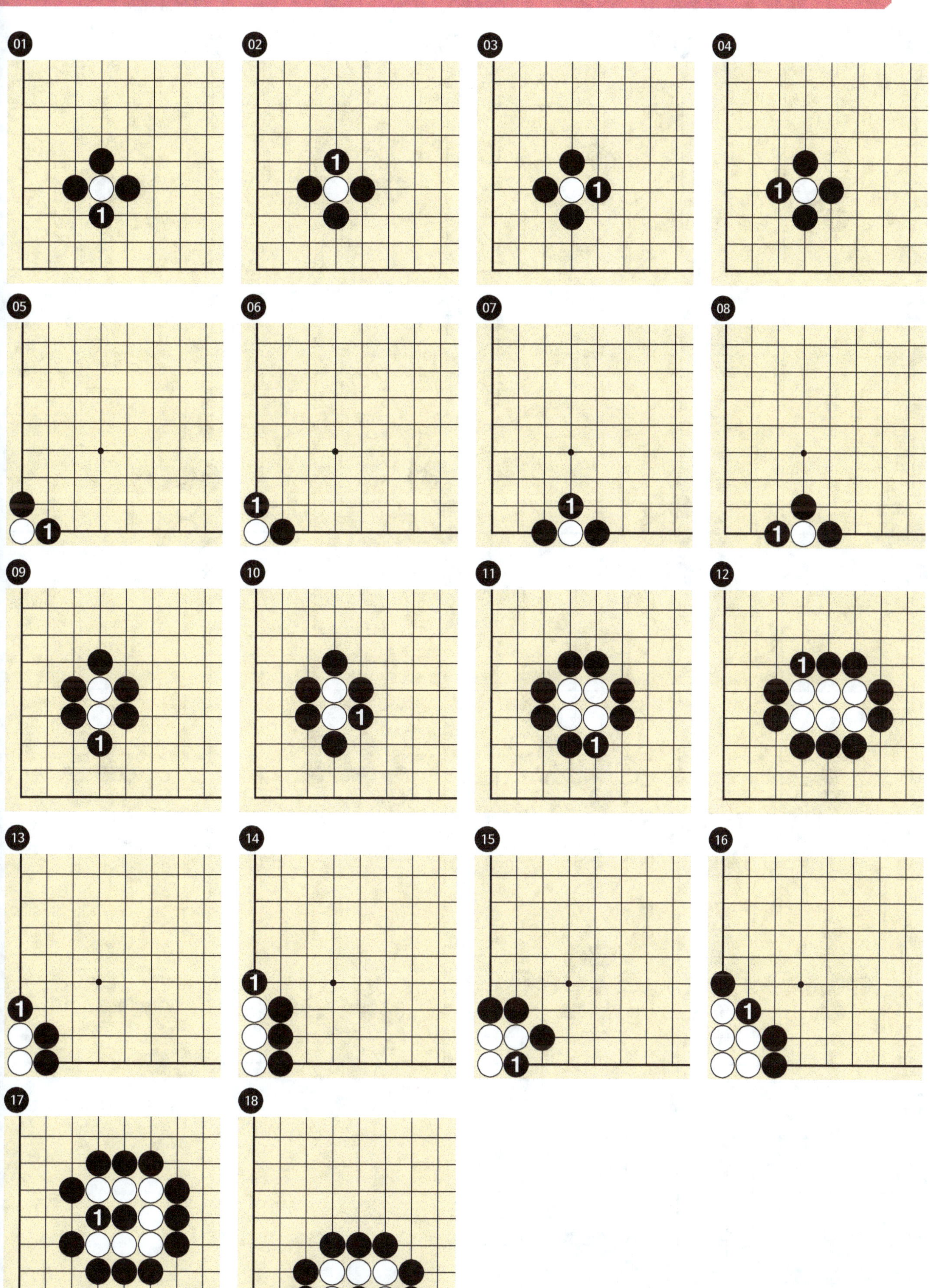

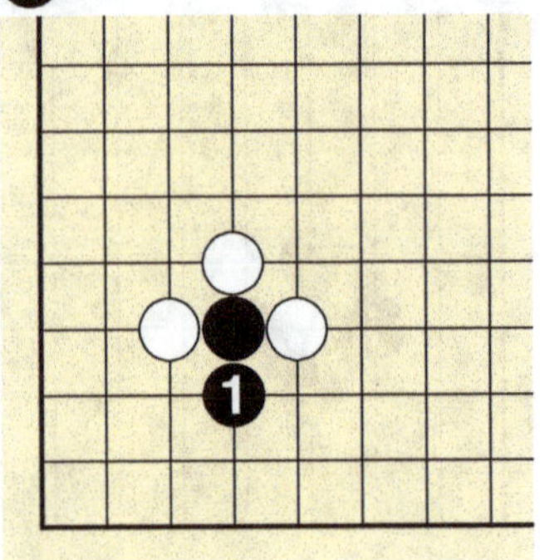

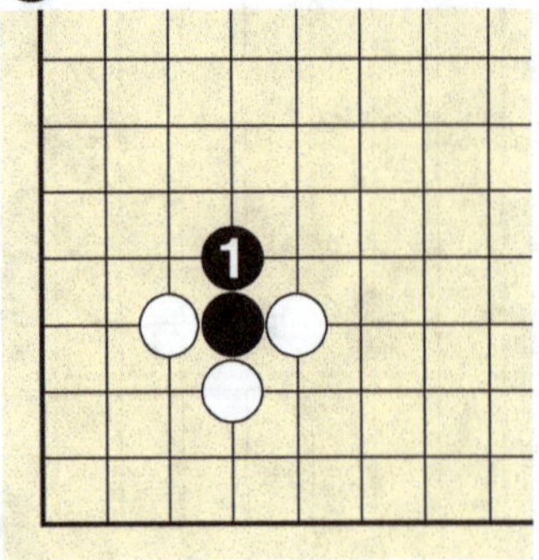

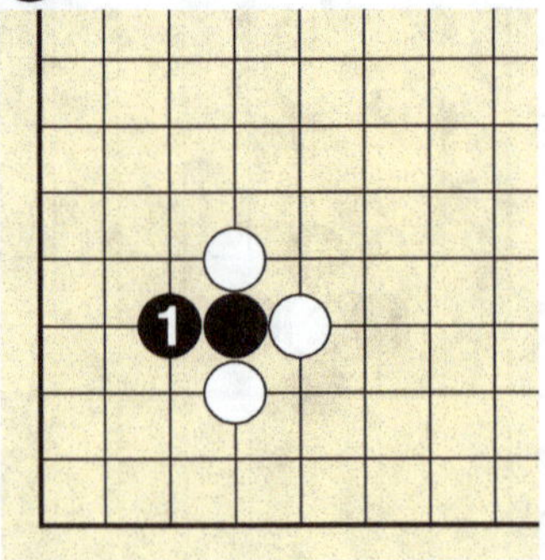

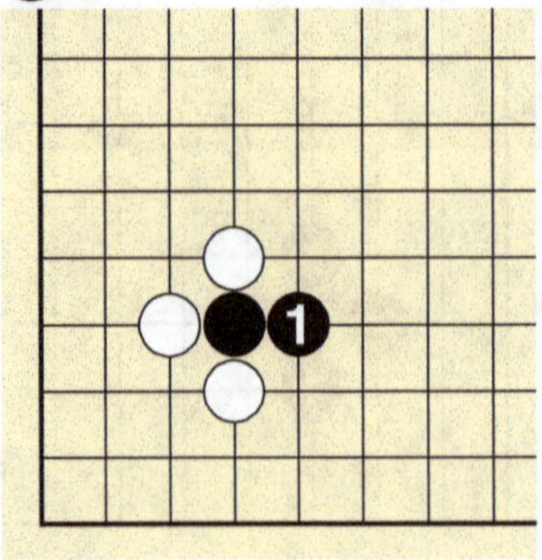

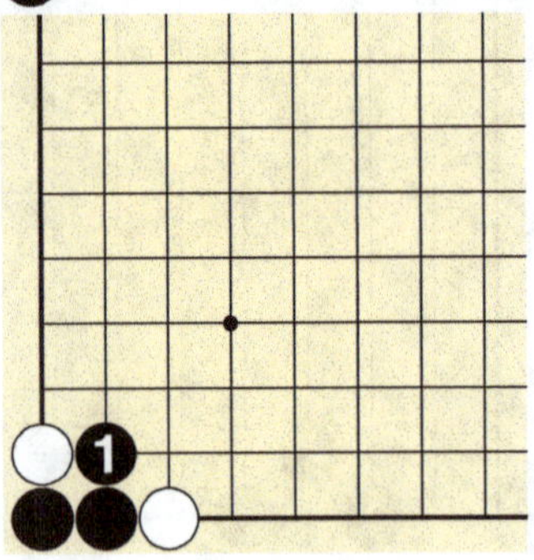

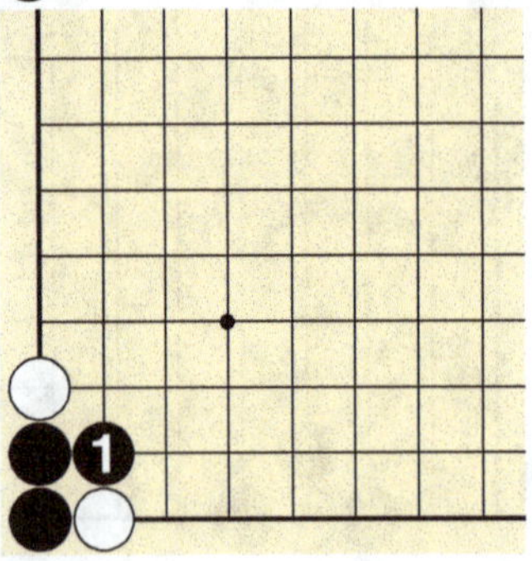

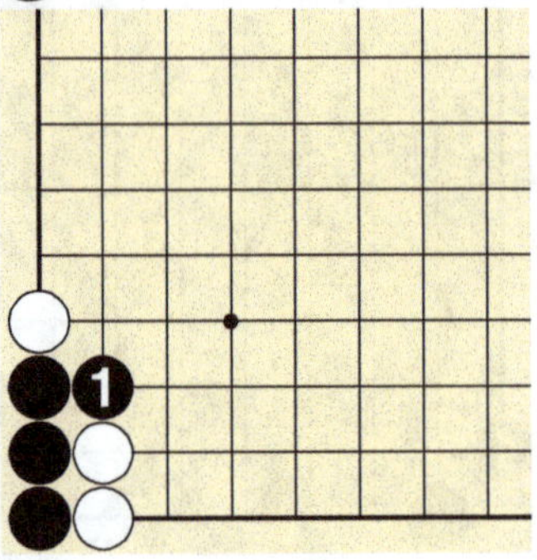

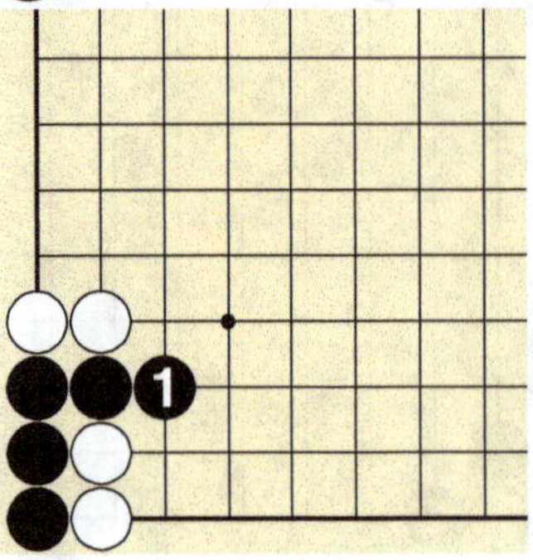

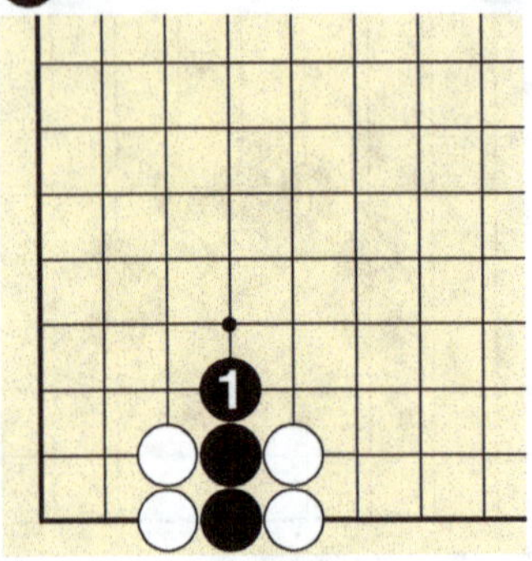

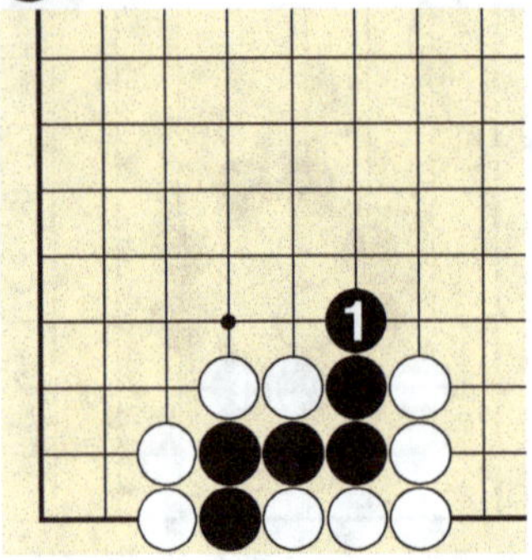

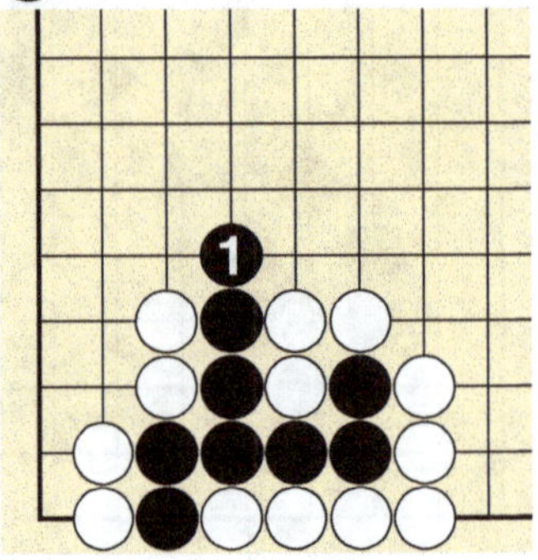

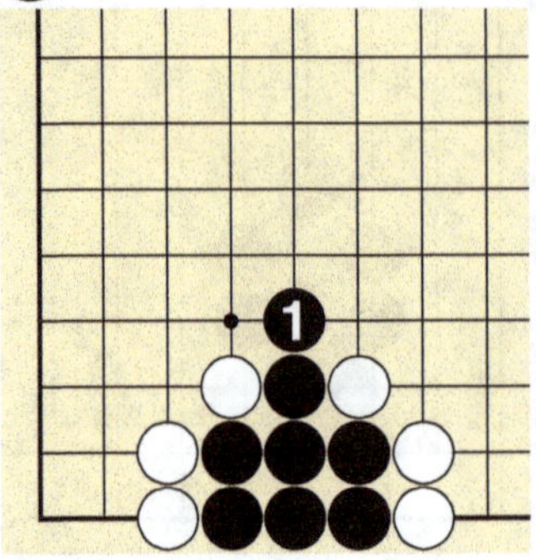

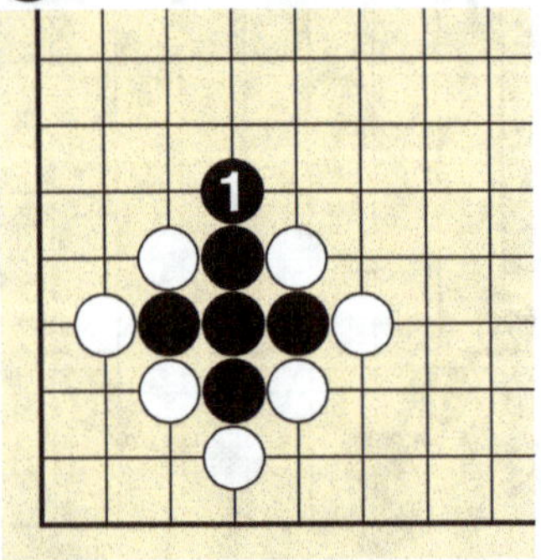

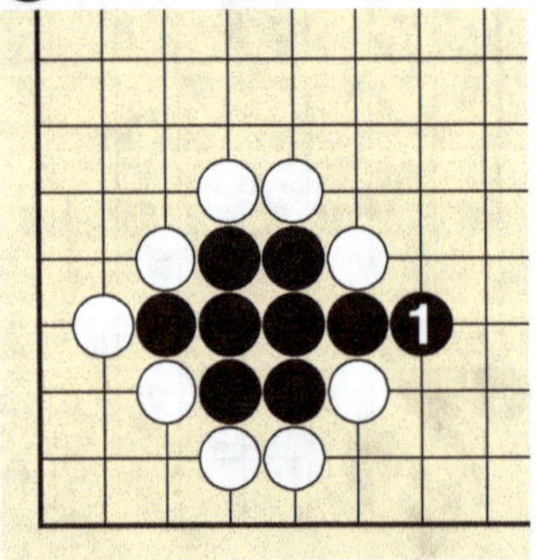

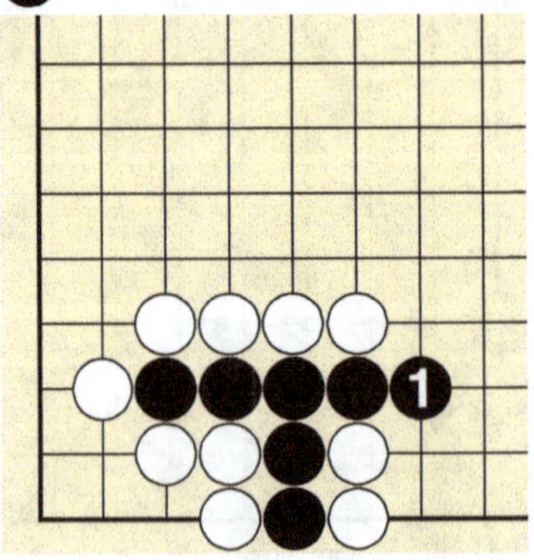

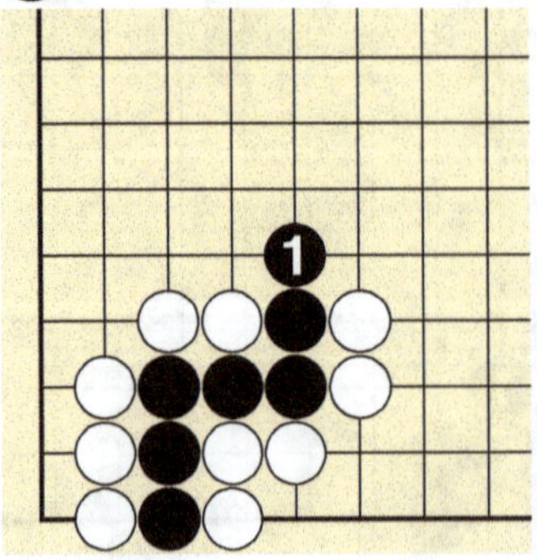

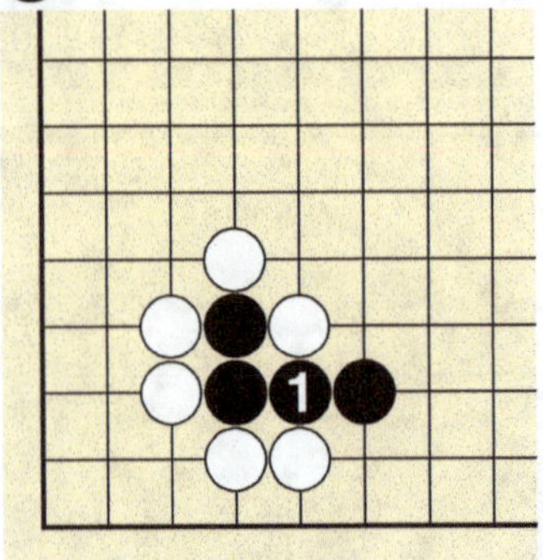

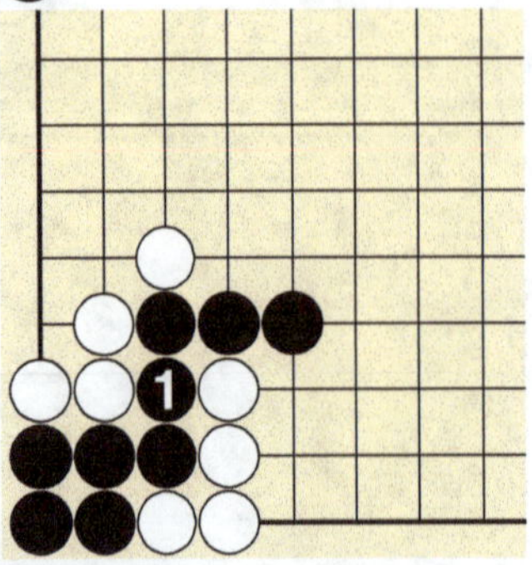

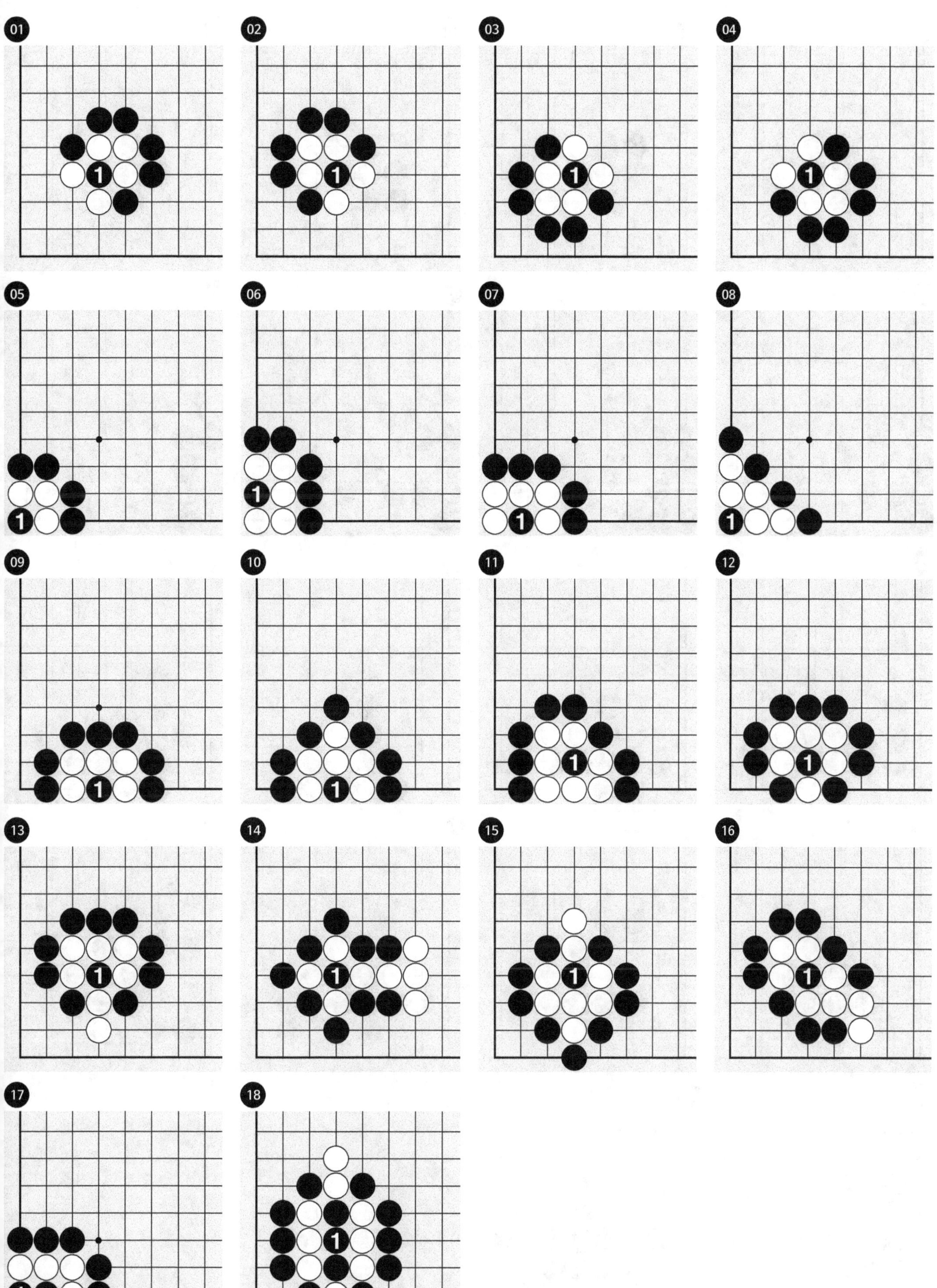

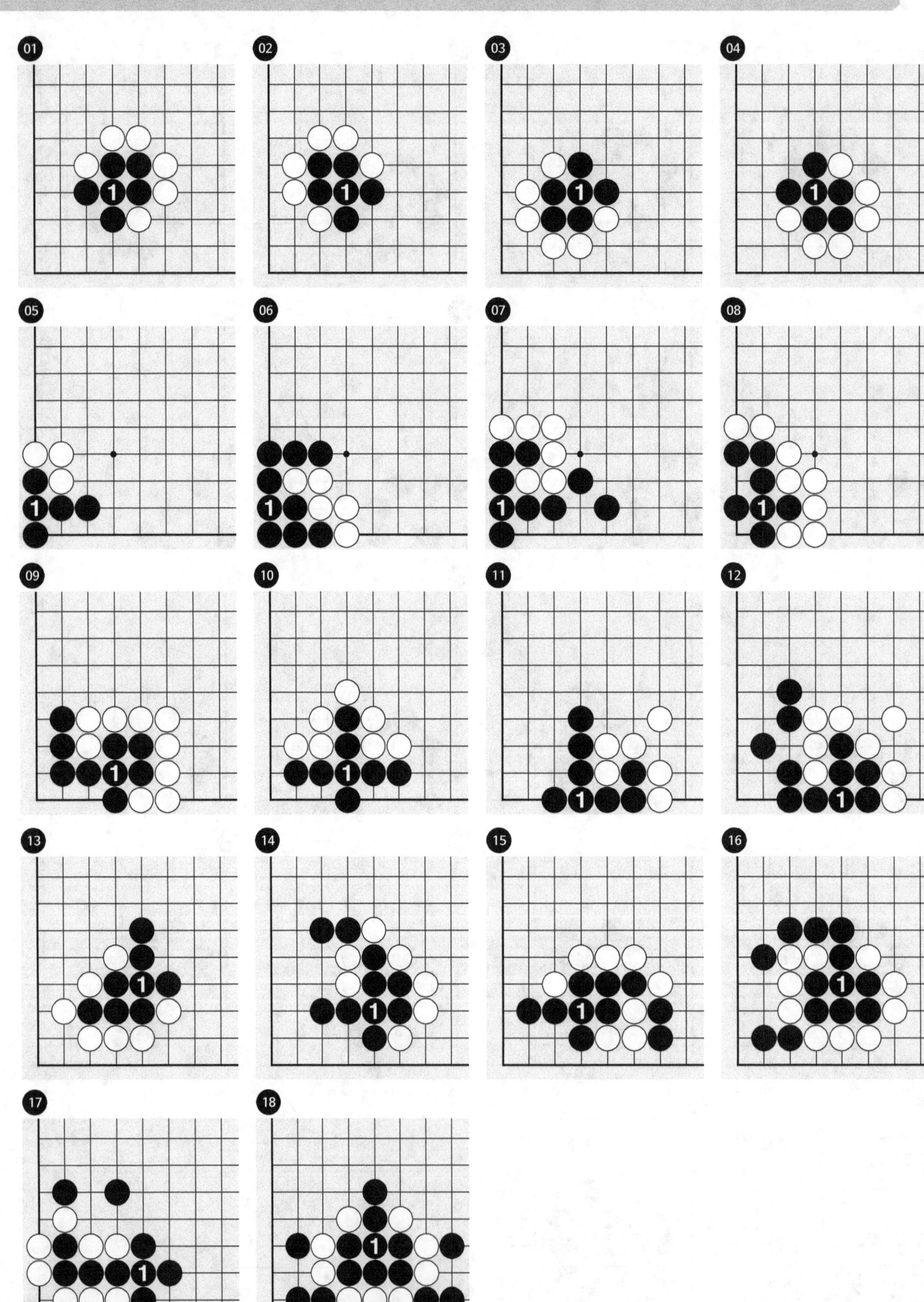

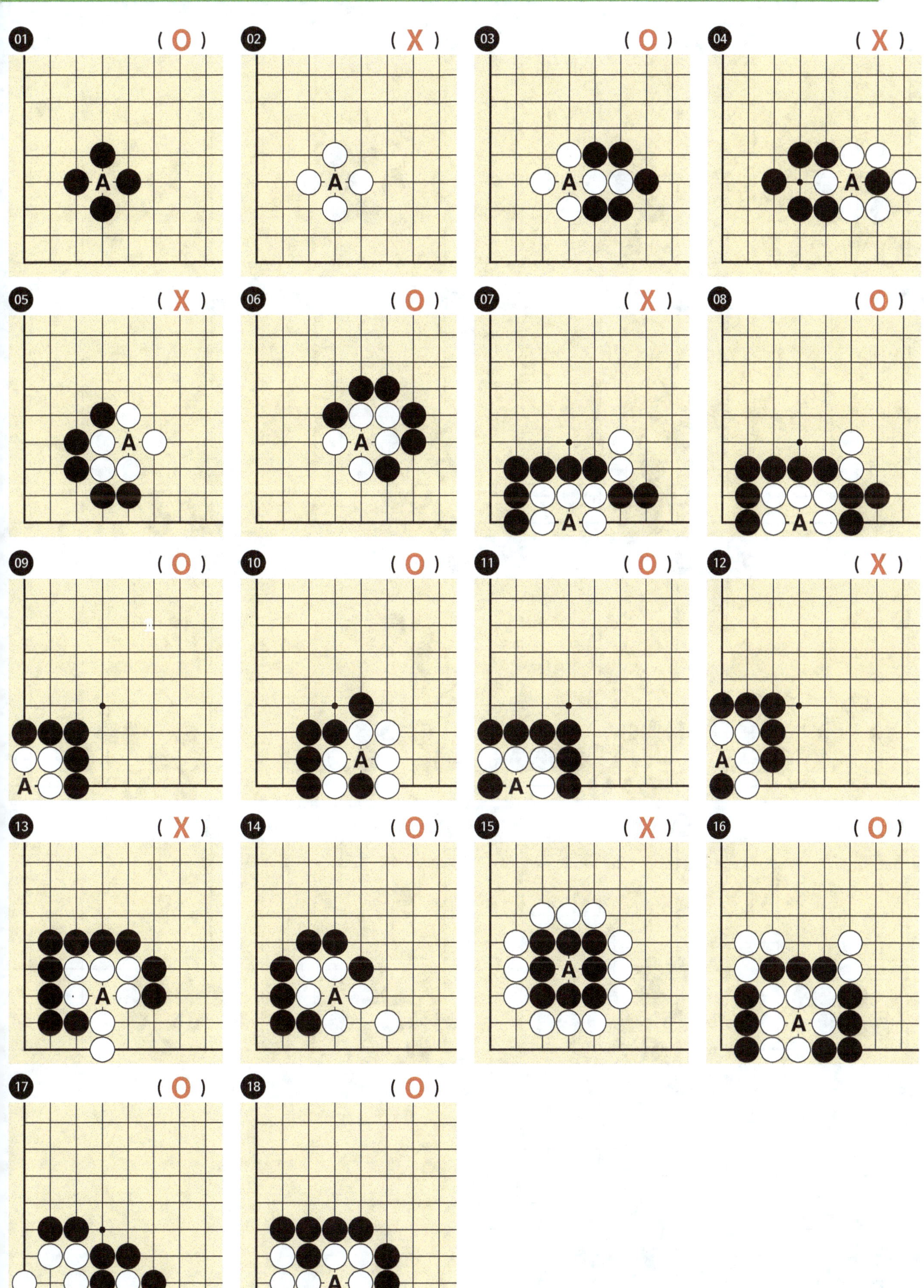
01 (O)
02 (X)
03 (O)
04 (X)
05 (X)
06 (O)
07 (X)
08 (O)
09 (O)
10 (O)
11 (O)
12 (X)
13 (X)
14 (O)
15 (X)
16 (O)
17 (O)
18 (O)

01 (O)	02 (X)	03 (X)	04 (O)
05 (O)	06 (O)	07 (X)	08 (X)
09 (O)	10	11	12
13	14	15	16
17	18		

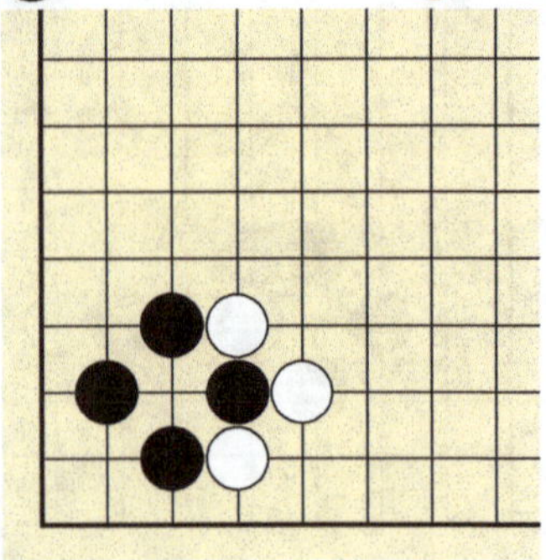

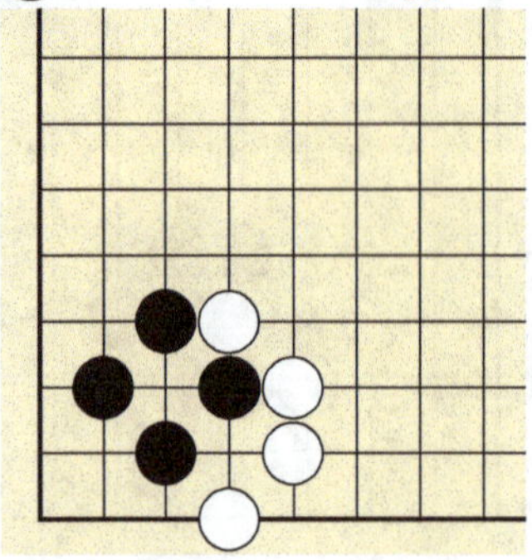

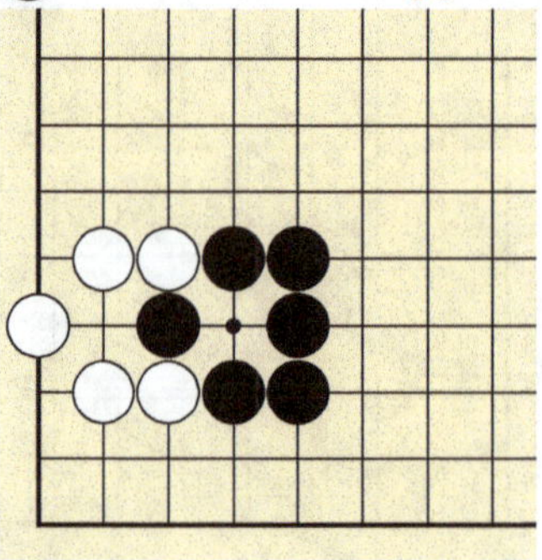

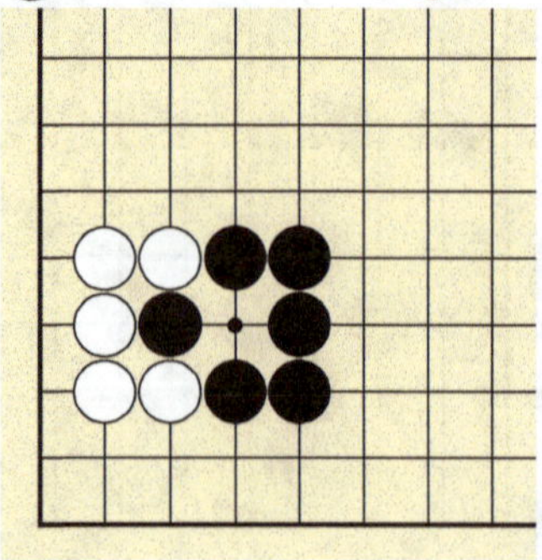

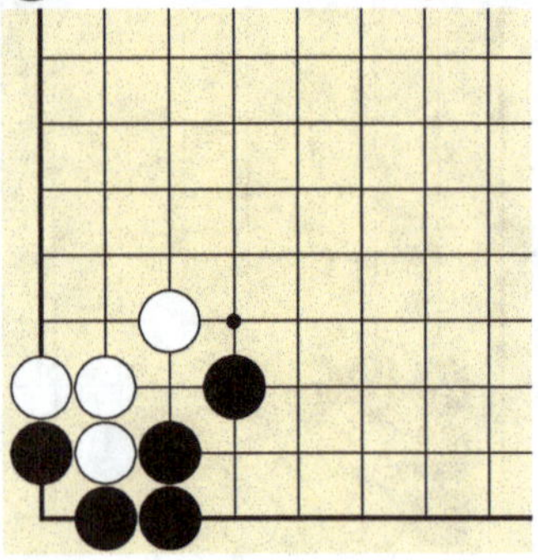

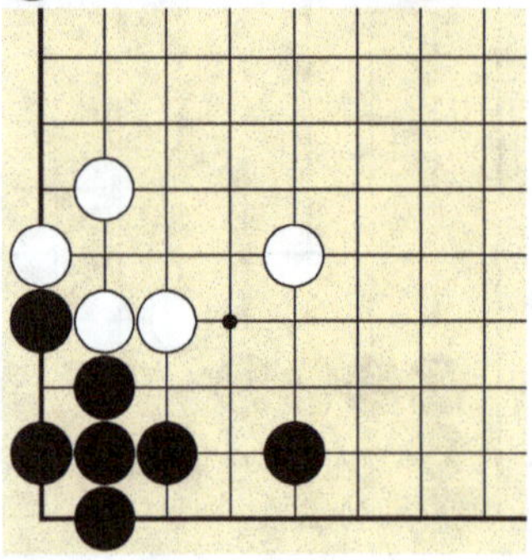

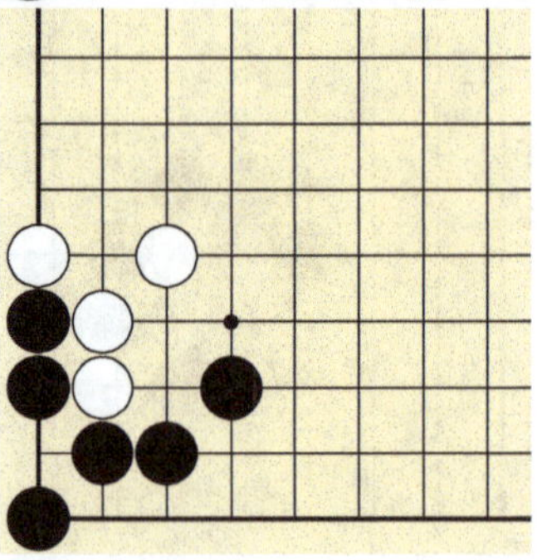

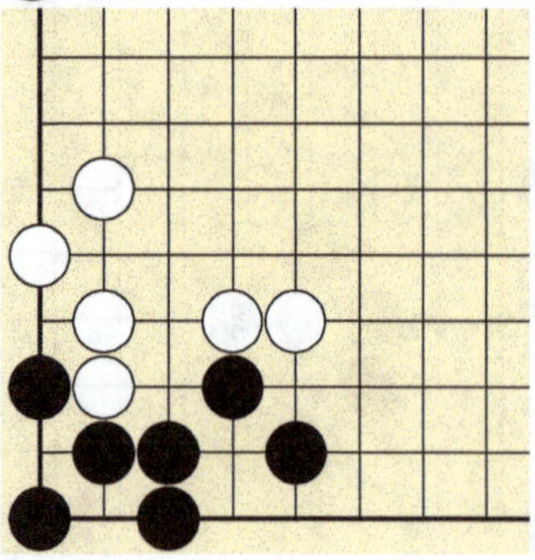

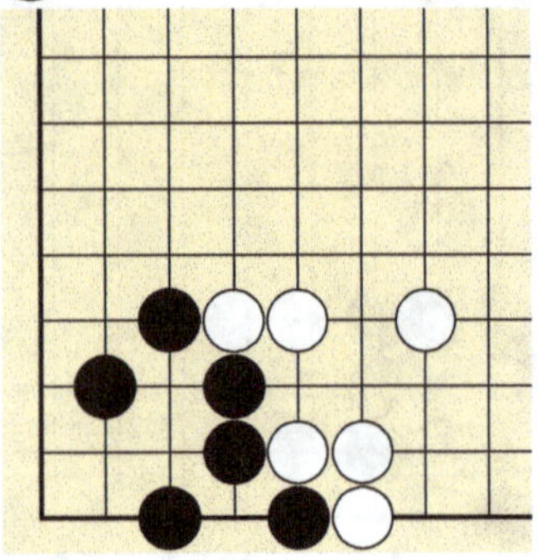

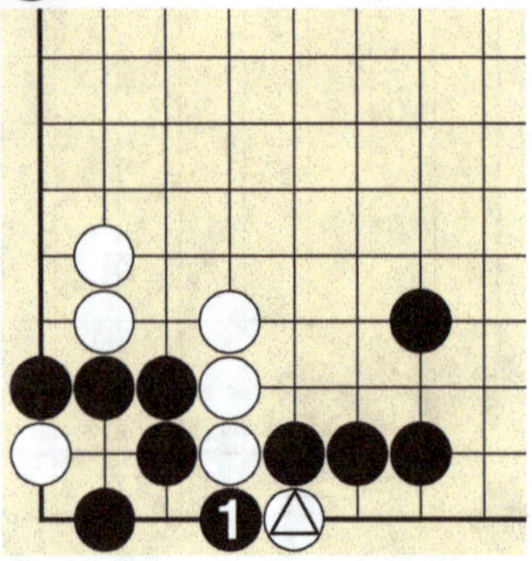

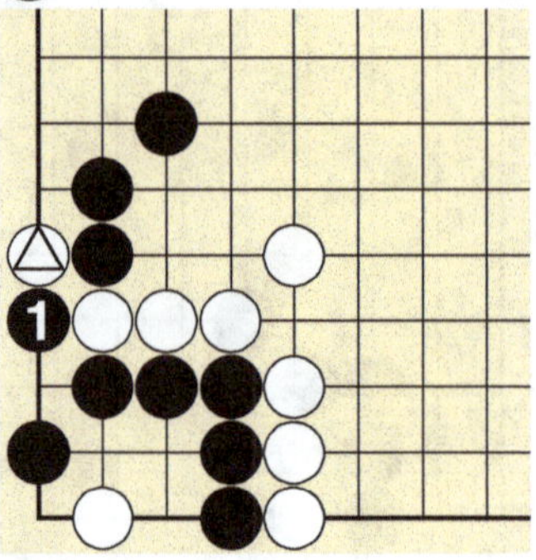

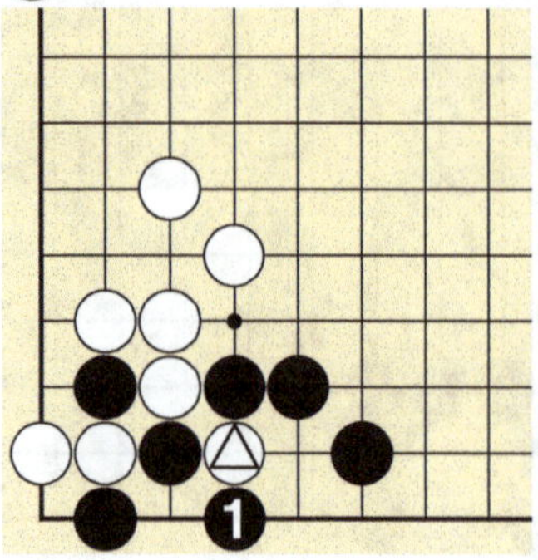

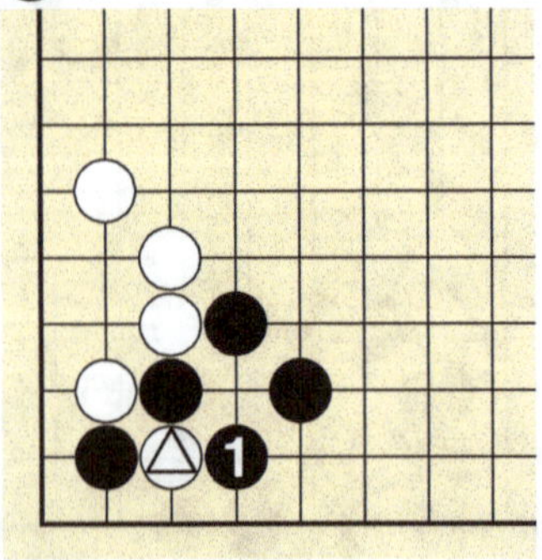

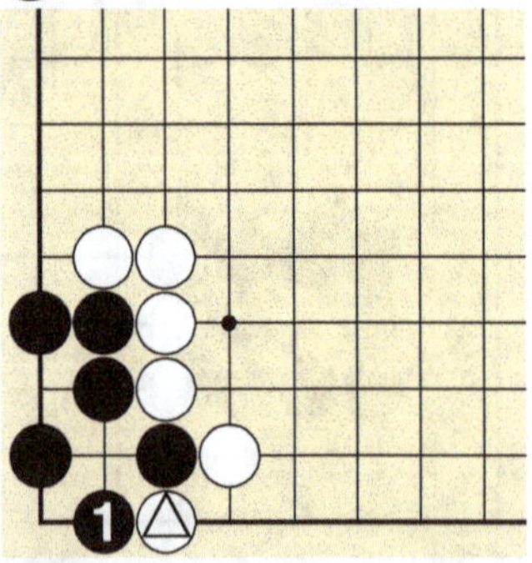

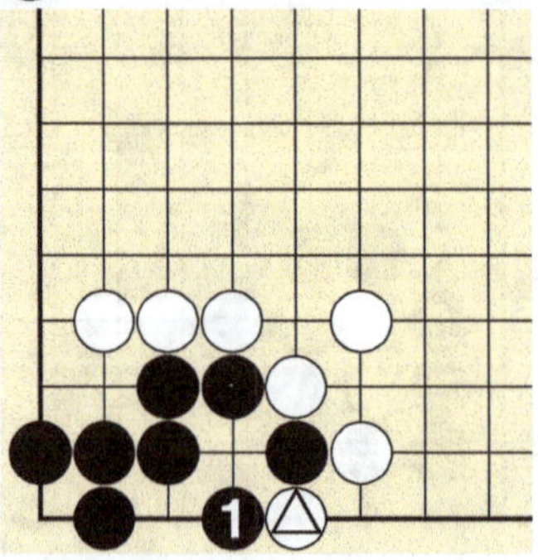

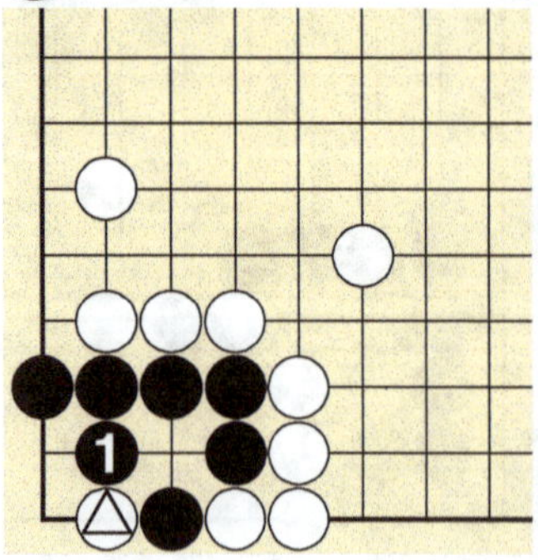

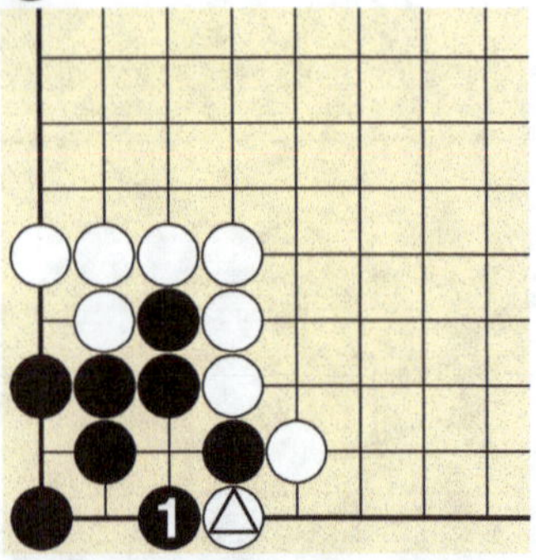

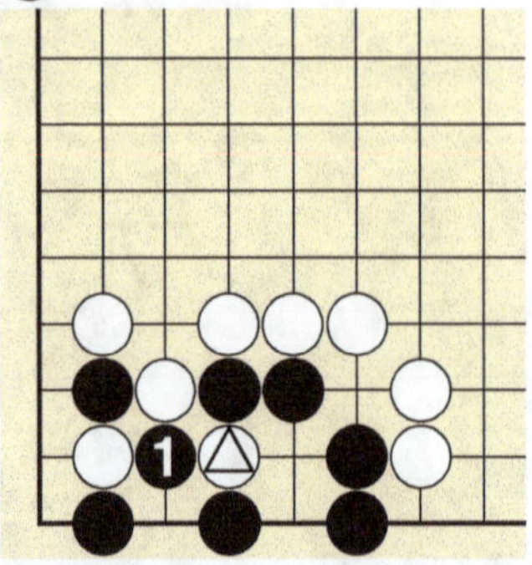

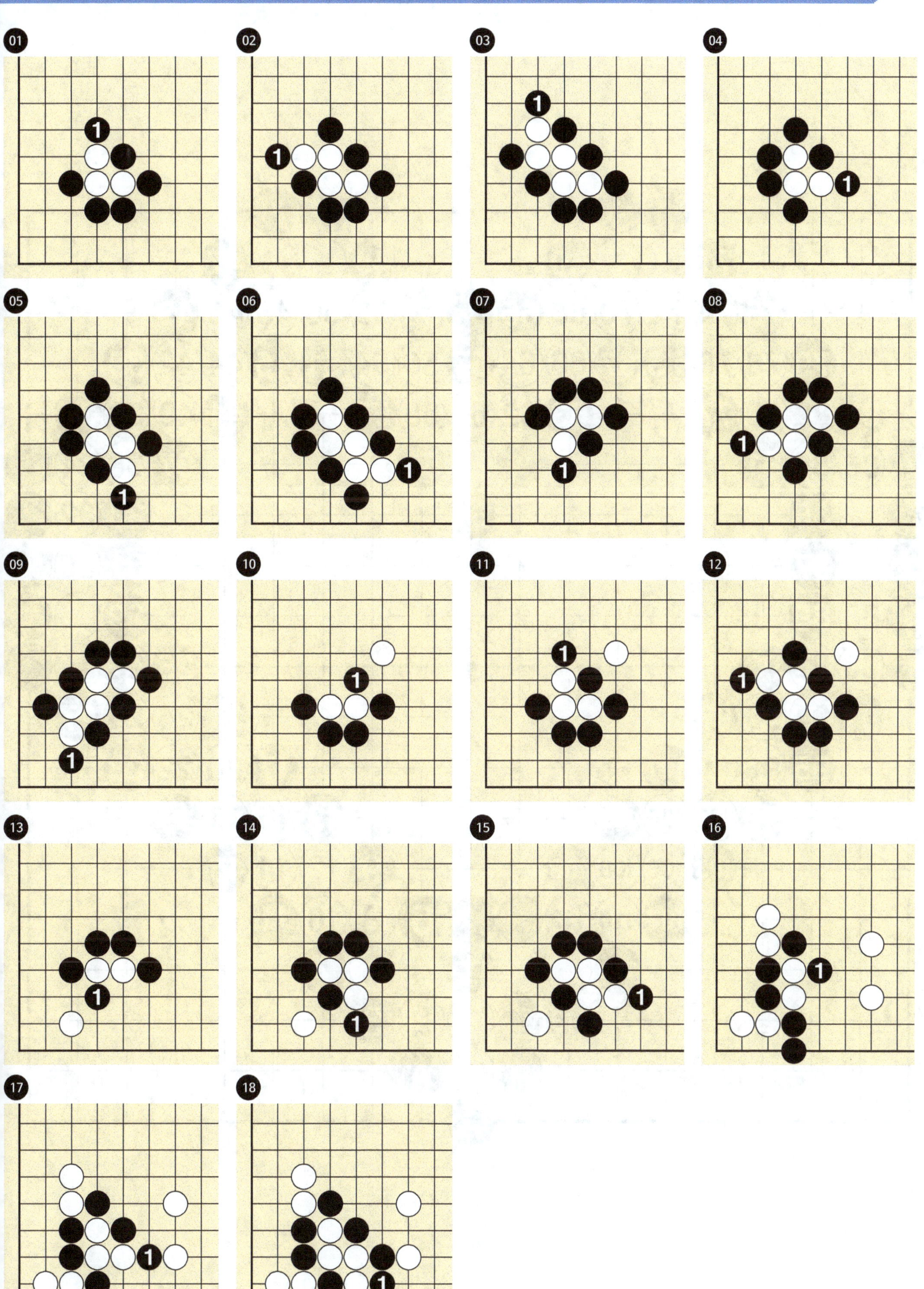

01

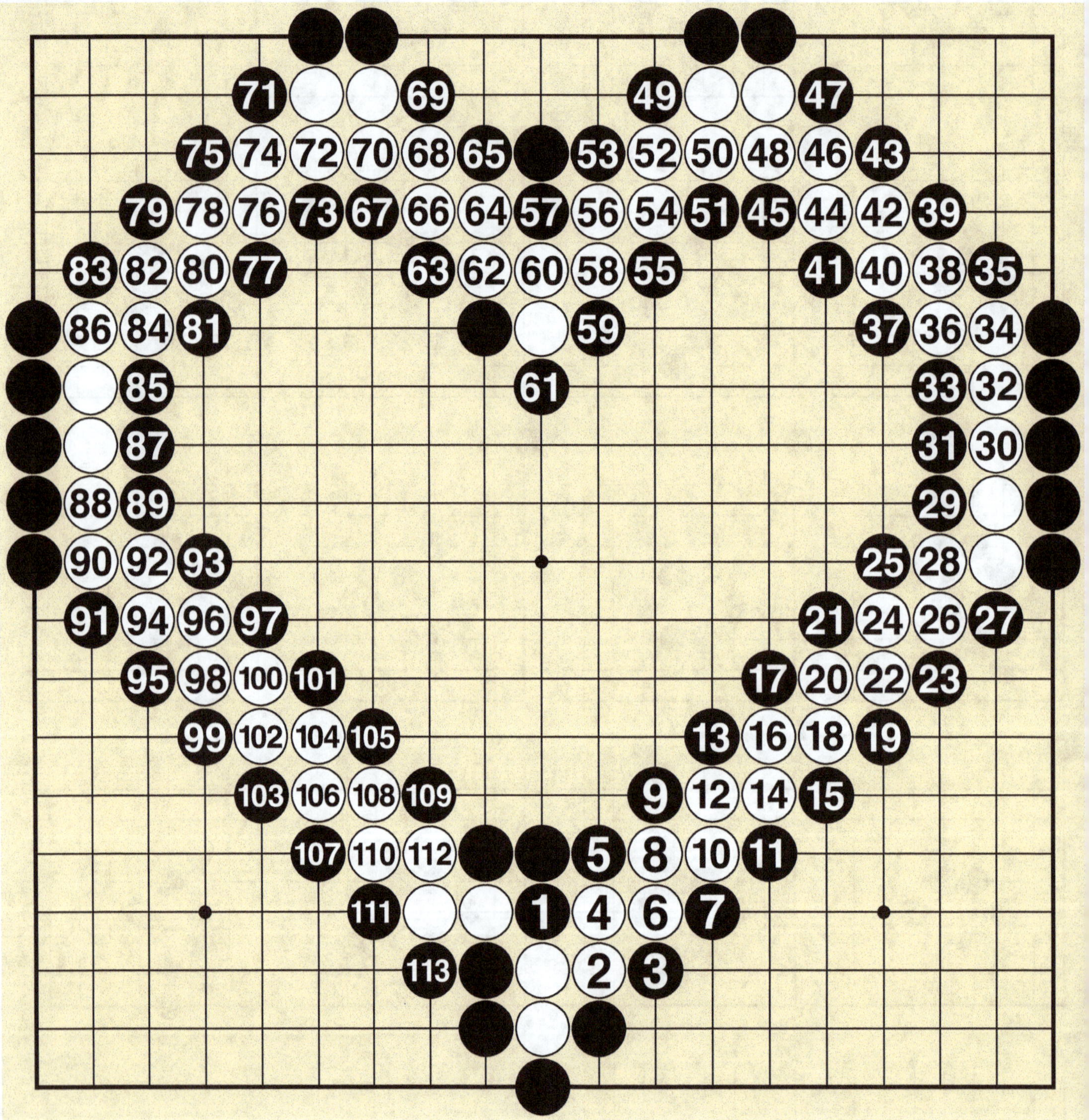

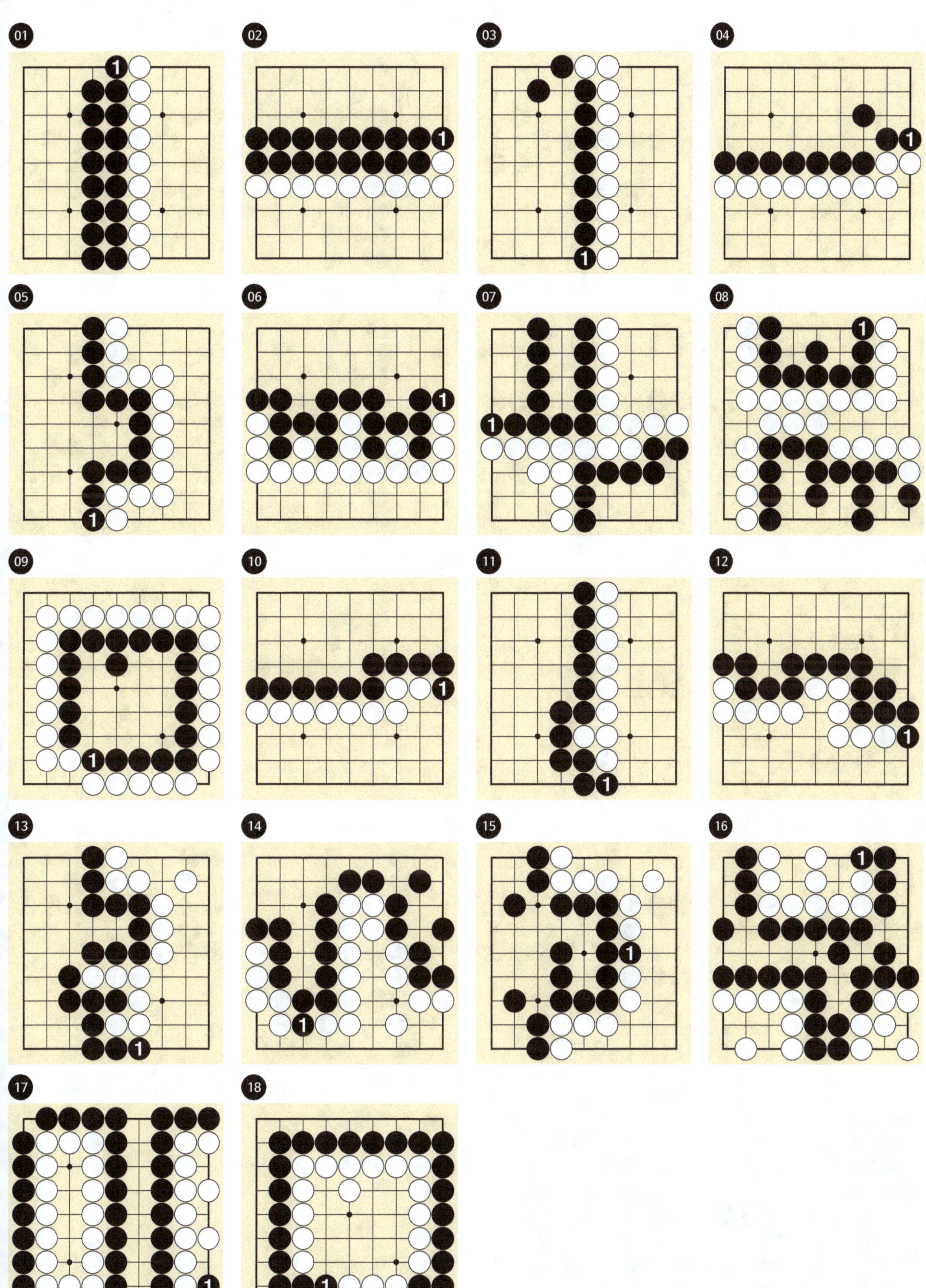

01

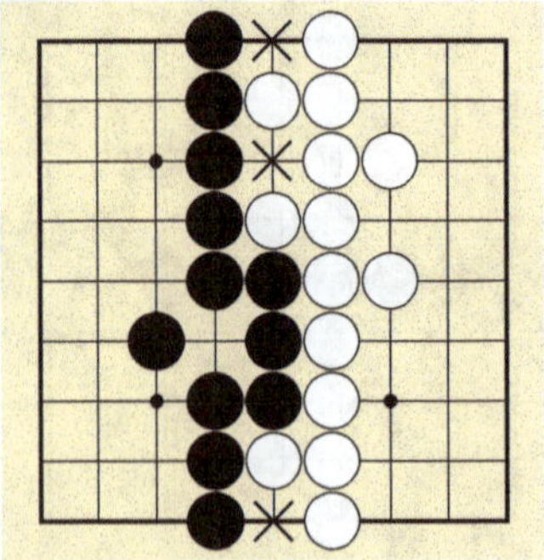

02

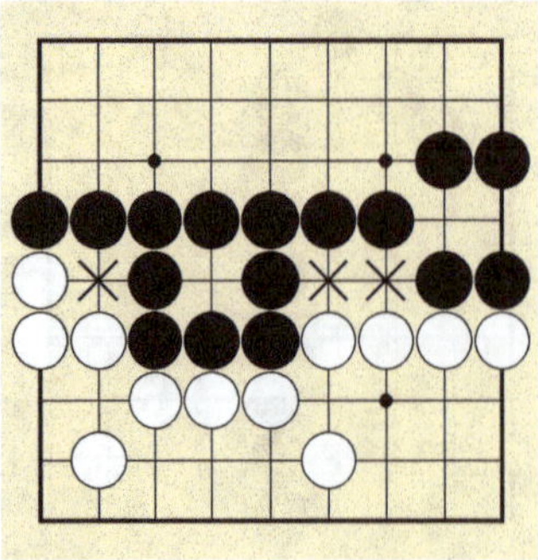

03

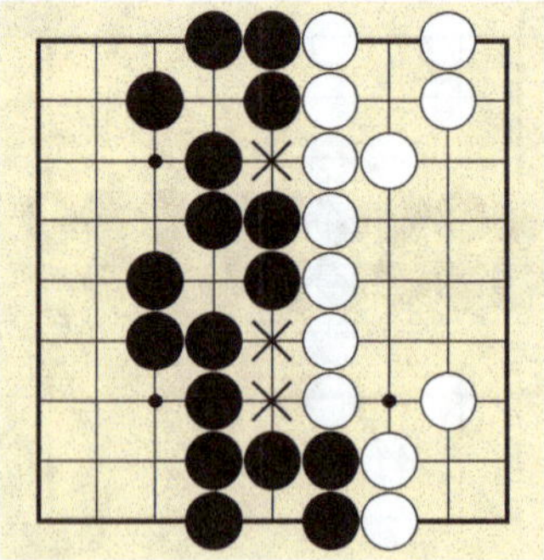

04

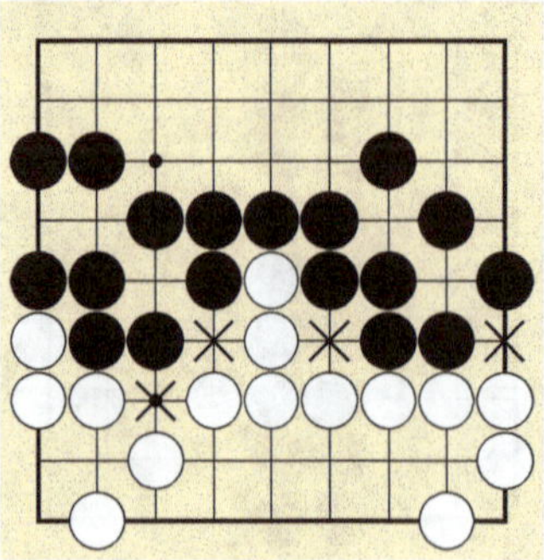

05

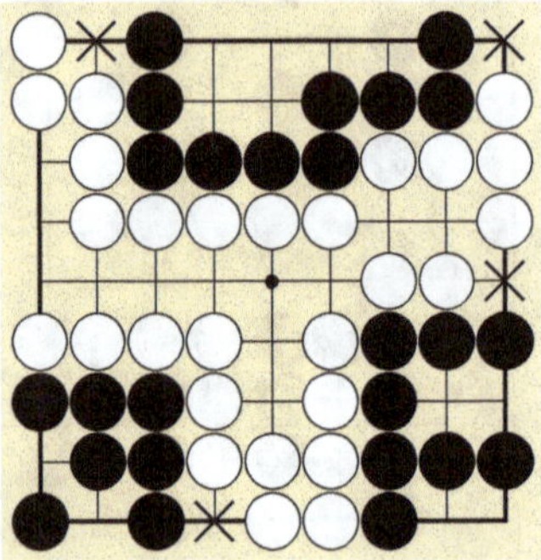

06

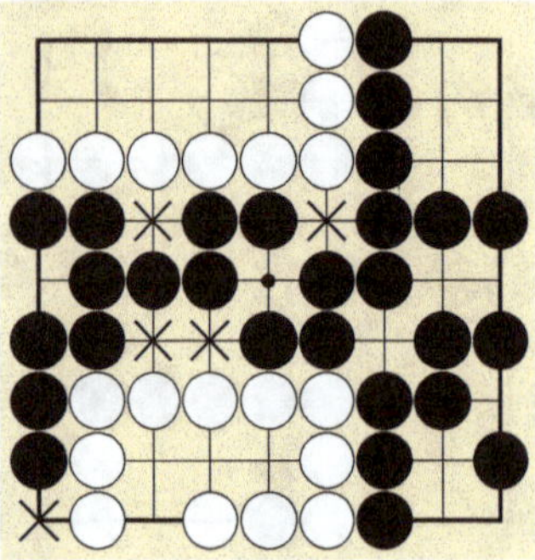

07

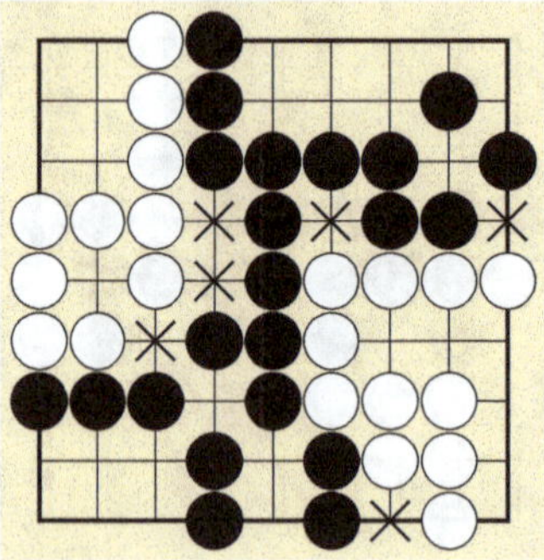

08

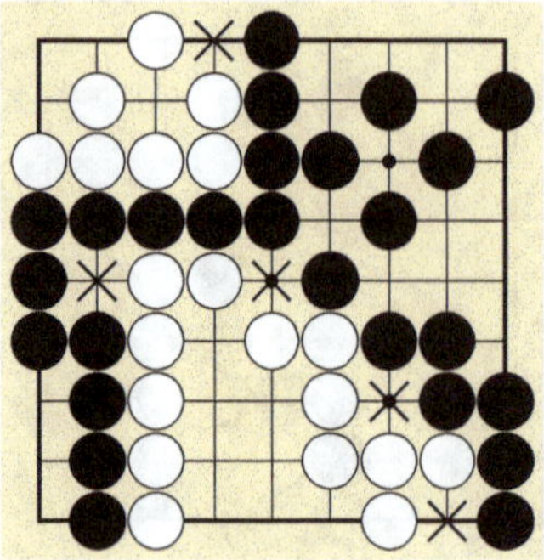

09

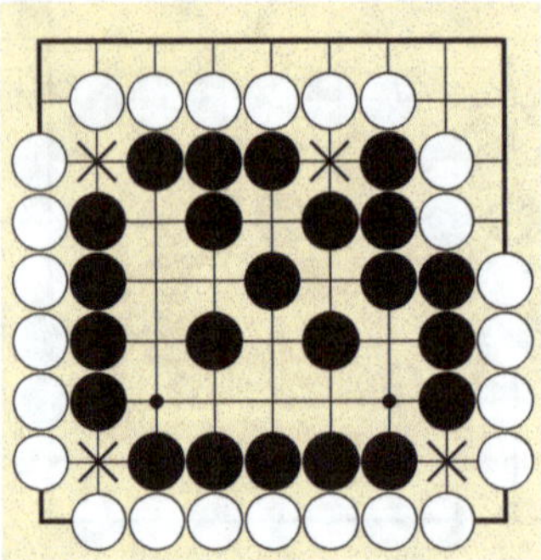

10

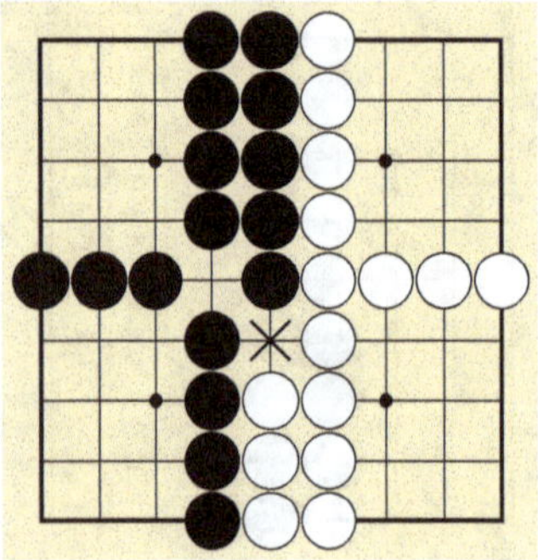

11

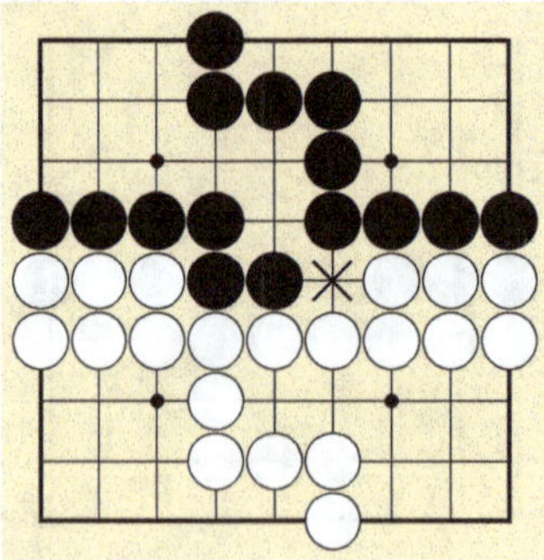

12

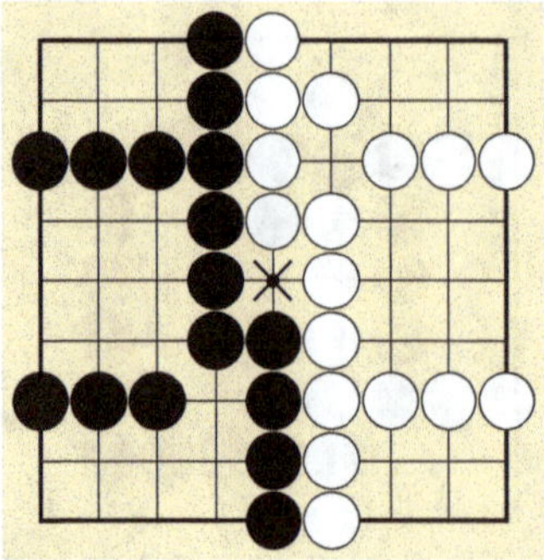

13

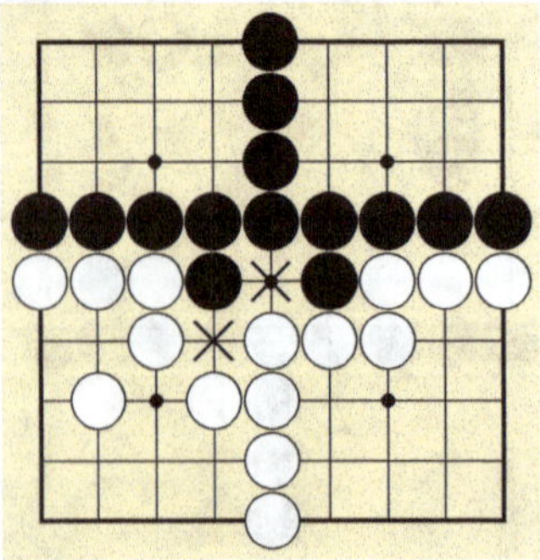

14

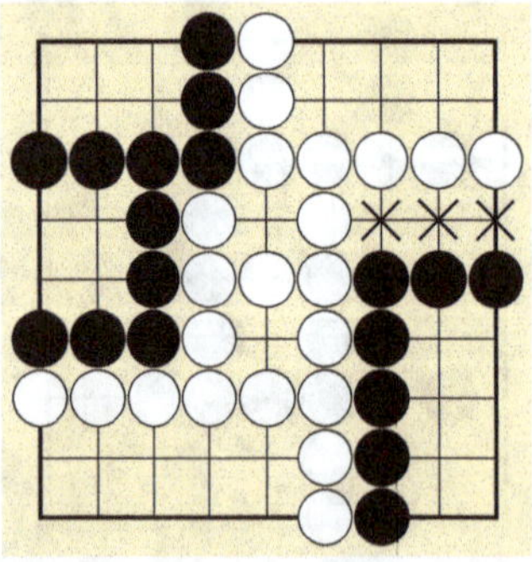

15

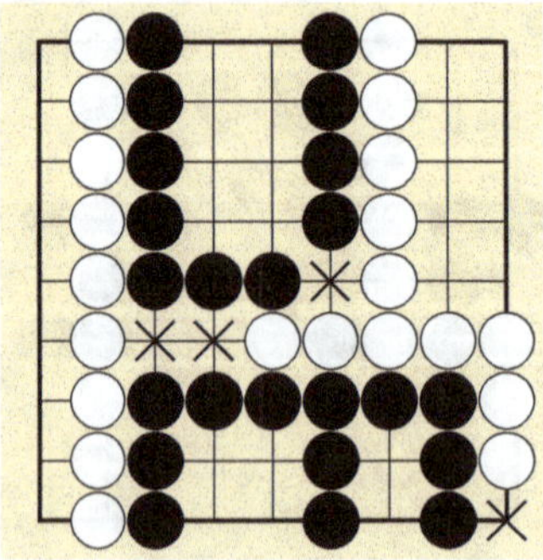

16

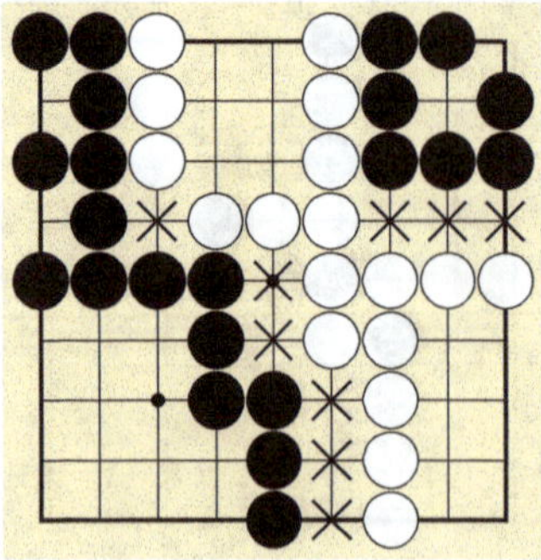

17

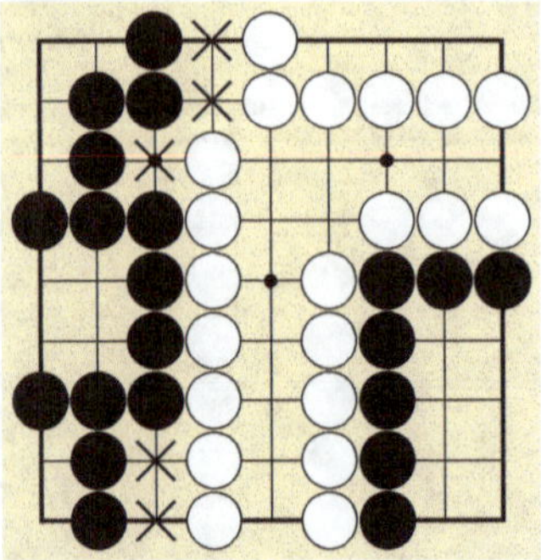

18

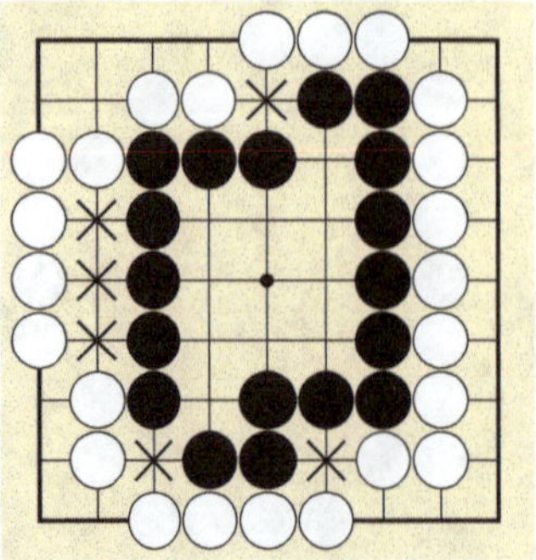